NANCY JOHNSON-SREBRO

block magic

Over 50 Fun & Easy Blocks from Squares and Rectangles

C&T PUBLISHING

©2001 Silver Star, Inc.
Illustrations ©2001 C&T Publishing

Editor: Liz Aneloski
Technical Editor: Sara Kate MacFarland
Copy Editor: Carol Barrett
Design Director/Book Designer: Aliza Kahn Shalit
Cover Design: Aliza Kahn Shalit
Production Coordinator: Diane Pedersen
Production Assistant: Stacy Chamness and Tim Manibusan
Quilt Photographer: Sharon Risedorph
Illustrator: Kandy Petersen

Published by C&T Publishing, Inc. P.O. Box 1456, Lafayette, California 94549

Attention Teachers:
C&T Publishing, Inc. encourages you to use this book as a text for teaching. Contact us at
800-284-1114 or www.ctpub.com for more information about the C&T Teachers Program.

Library of Congress Cataloging-in-Publication Data

Johnson-Srebro, Nancy.
  Block magic : over 50 fun & easy blocks made from squares and
rectangles / Nancy Johnson-Srebro.
      p. cm.
  ISBN 1-57120-120-3
  1. Patchwork—Patterns. 2. Quilting—Patterns. I. Title.
  TT835 .J586 2000
  746.46'041—dc21
                        00-010377

10 9 8 7 6 5 4 3 2 1

Dedication

This book is dedicated to Frank: my husband, friend, and partner.
Thank you for your love, guidance, patience, and support over the years.
Many things are possible with you at my side.

ACKNOWLEDGMENTS

There were dozens of people who supported me in various ways during the two years it took to write this book. A "thank-you" hardly seems adequate for everyone, so I'd like to extend special thanks to the following people:

My children, Mark, Alan, and Karen, whose love and support mean the world to me. Each of you has grown into a fine, responsible adult, and I'm proud of you!

My granddaughter, Casey, who brought a peaceful light into my world and joy to my heart. She spent hours identifying each block as I would sew them. If she didn't know what the block was supposed to be, I knew it was time to go back to the drawing board!

My mother, Ruby Johnson, who taught me not to give up on projects, special thanks for spending hours whip-stitching the bindings on the quilts.

Ruth Lindhagen, Janet McCarroll, Cindy Mundy Cochran, and Erena Rieflin, who willingly gave much effort over the two years to design and proof patterns and Quilt Maps, as well as to sew samples. They were invaluable to say the least.

A special thanks to a great group of machine quilters: Brenda Leino from Plaid Farm Quilting, MN; Marcia Stevens from Little Pine Studio, MN; and Lea Wang from Custom Machine Quilting, NJ. All three are true professionals who met every commitment and deadline, no matter what. I can't thank them enough.

Karen Brown and Georgia Adamitis, for over twenty years of friendship, love, and support.

Bonnie Campbell and Marcia Rickansrud, for their strong faith, support, and compassion.

Members of the "Always In Stitches" group: Vicki Novajosky, Arlene Shea, Roxanne Sidorek, Sandy Storz. Your opinions and honesty are always appreciated.

Trish Katz and Janet Levin, whose sense of humor brought a smile during some busy times.

Todd Hensley of C&T Publishing; my editors, Liz Aneloski and Sara MacFarland; and many others on the C&T Staff for their friendship, attention to detail, and quality of work.

Many companies have supported me for years and supplied products for this book.

Special thanks are extended to:
- American & Efird and Marci Brier for Mettler and Signature threads
- Benartex, Inc. for fabric
- Bernina of America for 170 Series Bernina® sewing machine
- P&B Textiles and Sharon Johnson for fabric
- Prym Dritz®/Omnigrid® for notions, rotary cutters, rulers and mats
- The Warm Company for batting and Steam-a-Steam 2

The following companies gave additional support for this book:
- Fabric Sales Co., Inc. for fabric
- Fairfield Processing Corporation for batting
- Robert Kaufman for fabric
- Mission Valley Fabrics Division PCCA for fabric
- RJR Fashion Fabrics for fabric
- The Stearns Technical Textiles Company for batting
- Wrights for notions

CONTENTS

Cool Cat   12

Tulips Galore   13

Ballerina   14

Schoolhouse   16

Snow Family   17

Sewing Machine   18

Scaredy-Cat   19

Angel of Love   20

Pinwheel Flowers   21

School Bus   22

Max   23

Locomotive   24

Birdhouse   26

Hot Air Balloon   27

Magic Watering Can 28

Ruff the Dog   29

Freddy the Frog   30

Samantha   31

Campbell's Beach
House   32

Patches the Cow   34

Nutcracker   35

Noah's Ark   36

Toy Horse   37

The Homestead   38

Country Cottage   39

INTRODUCTION

Greetings to quilters everywhere!

I've always done things a little differently than most people. Whenever I hear something like "that can't be done," I'm ready to find a way to do it! One of my heroes is Ralph Waldo Emerson who said it well, "Do not go where the path may lead, go instead where there is no path and leave a trail." I feel this is what I've done with this book.

I had a clear idea of what I wanted to share with quilters—tons of original, No-Fail®, rotary cut patterns in four different sizes; lots of color photos to show how to personalize your blocks; easy sewing instructions; and many different Quilt Maps™ to use for setting the blocks together. As a quilter, I've always searched for quilt books that would give me options, and I wanted this book to meet that goal.

Virtually all the blocks in this book are original designs that are presented to quilters for the first time. As you look through the pages that follow, you may be surprised to find that all the blocks and Quilt Maps™ can be made using only TWO rotary cut shapes—a square and a rectangle! These two basic shapes are stitched together to create triangles and more complicated shapes and will provide you with hours of sewing fun. Once you start working with these shapes, you'll be able to come up with some original blocks of your own!

Some people say it's a labor of love, but the process of writing a book of this scope is long and hard with many tribulations along the way. There are some experiences and benefits I hold dear; among these are the friendships I've formed and the joy of working with creative people. Book writing is never a one-person operation. In this regard I was fortunate to work with a truly wonderful group of pattern proofers, professional machine quilters, C&T Publishing staff, manufacturers, my family, and friends. Each and every person played an important role in getting this book to you.

There's nothing like sitting down with a new quilting book and oohing and aahing over all the color photos and quilt patterns. So, sit back in a favorite chair, grab a cup of coffee or candy bar, and start dreaming of your next quilt.

Nancy

HOW TO READ THE CHARTS

Letter refers to the specific piece noted in the block illustration.

Finished shape and color as it relates to the featured block.

Number of squares or rectangles to cut.

Block sizes to choose from.

USED FOR	SHAPE/ COLOR	NUMBER TO CUT	BLOCK SIZE			
			6"	8"	10"	12"
A	☐	1 ☐	3½	4½	5½	6½
B	◹	4 ☐	2	2½	3	3½
C	▨ ◹	48 ▨	1¼	1½	1¾	2
D	◢	4 ▬	1½ X 2	1¾ X 2¼	2 X 2½	2¼ X 2¾

Measurements are given in inches.
Single measurements indicate the size of a cut square (2 = 2" x 2").

THE BASICS

ROTARY CUTTING EQUIPMENT

I believe the type of equipment you use for quiltmaking makes the difference in how good the finished quilt will look. Use accurately printed rulers, such as Omnigrid® products, and a good quality cutting mat, such as Omnigrid mat or Dritz® Dura-Heal Cutting Mat. Also, be sure the rotary cutter you use is suited for your particular needs. I've found the Dritz® 45mm Pressure-Sensitive rotary cutter allows me to rotary cut for hours without hand fatigue.

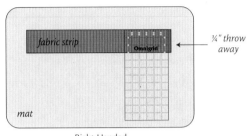

Right-Handed

ROTARY CUTTING INSTRUCTIONS

There are only two geometric shapes used in the patterns in this book—a square and a rectangle. Both are very easy to rotary cut. The following diagrams illustrate the cutting technique for a left-handed and a right-handed person.

Cutting a Square

Step One: The block instructions will indicate the cut height of the square. For example, the instructions require four 3" x 3" squares. Cut a strip of fabric 3" x 13". Always cut the strip a little longer than necessary; this will allow you to "square up" the short end of the strip. Place the short side of the ruler along the top of the strip. Square-up the short side of the strip by trimming approximately ¼" from the edge.

Step Two: After squaring up one end of the strip, turn the mat one-half turn (180 degrees). Place the ruler on top of the fabric so the 3" marking lines up with the newly cut edge. Be sure the top of the ruler is even with the top of the strip. Rotary cut.

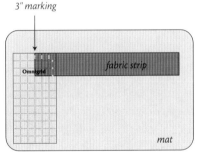

Left-Handed
STEP ONE

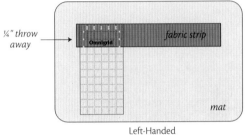

Right-Handed

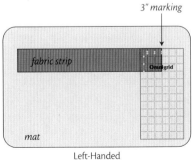

Left-Handed
STEP TWO

Cutting a Rectangle

Let's say the block instructions call for two 3" x 5" rectangles. Cut a strip of fabric 3" x 11". Square-up the short end of the strip as shown in Step One for cutting a square. Turn the mat half a turn. Next, place the ruler on top of the strip so the 5" marking lines up with the newly cut edge. Be sure the top of the ruler is even with the top of the strip. Rotary cut.

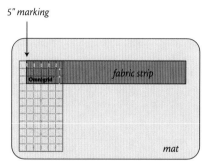
Right-Handed

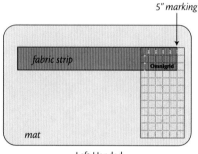
Left-Handed

FABRIC AND THREAD CHOICES

For best results, I encourage you to use good quality 100% cotton fabrics. You can find them at quilt shops throughout the world. If possible, pre-wash the fabrics before using them. This ensures that they are preshrunk and the dyes won't bleed if your block or quilt must be washed in the future.

I do all of my machine piecing with Mettler 100% cotton silk finish thread. The weight is 50/3. For almost all of my piecing I use a light beige color thread (color #703). However, when I sew on black fabric I use navy blue thread, and black thread when I sew on navy blue fabric. The slight difference between the thread and fabric colors is just enough to make it easy to rip out seams if necessary.

SEWING

No, this section is not going to be another technical summary of basic sewing techniques, at least not in the usual way. Most of you already know how to sew for quiltmaking. If you need a refresher course on the basics, choose one of the many great reference books available on the subject or other similar books that include basic quilting instructions.

One of the joys you discover while piecing the blocks in this book is that it's all straight stitching; no back tacking, no set-in seams, and no bias edges to deal with. You may even want to do some strip piecing if you're going to use the same fabrics and make several identical blocks.

I recommend that you lay out all of the block pieces on a small rigid surface before sewing the block together. This way you will be able to move the block to the sewing machine easily and will help prevent sewing errors.

I also want to share some special hints and tips that will help you build on your sewing skills. When you start making original blocks, no matter how much you have sewn, problems can arise. By following the suggestions in this section you can avoid most, if not all, of these.

Seam Allowance

I find it's best to use a scant ¼" seam allowance when quilt piecing. Using a scant seam allowance ensures the units/blocks are true to size because I regain the small amount of fabric that is lost due to the thickness of the sewing thread and the resulting "hump" that's created by pressing the seam allowances to one direction.

Hints for Sewing on the Diagonal

Let me share some hints for sewing the diagonal seams shown in this book. They will give you perfect piecing results every time.

1 Some of the squares and rectangles require you to draw a thin pencil line diagonally through the piece in order to sew it to the next piece. DO NOT sew precisely on the drawn pencil line. You should sew one or two threads to the right of it. This ensures the piece will be the correct size after pressing. If you sew exactly on the pencil line, the piece will likely be too small after pressing.

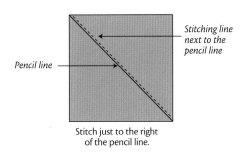

Stitching line next to the pencil line

Pencil line

Stitch just to the right of the pencil line.

2 Use a mechanical pencil with a lead no more than 0.5mm in diameter for drawing diagonal lines on your fabric. Don't use a regular pencil. It will become dull very quickly and the pencil line will be wider and bolder than desired.

3 Keep sharp needles in your sewing machine. A dull needle will distort the stitches. I use a 70/10 Jeans/Denim by Schmetz for all of my machine piecing.

4 A single-hole throat/stitch plate is also helpful. It will keep the needle from pushing the corner of the square into the zigzag throat/stitch plate hole (which has a larger opening).

5 When sewing diagonally through a square or rectangle, start sewing on a scrap piece of fabric first, then sew into the adjacent square/rectangle. This will help prevent distortion of the first one or two stitches.

6 Do your piecing with an open-toe walking foot. This will allow you to see where to sew NEXT to the pencil line. I do all of my machine piecing on a Bernina® 170 with an open-toe walking foot.

7 The needle-stop down feature on my sewing machine is very helpful when chain piecing. Use this feature if your machine has it.

8 Press the diagonally sewn seam FIRST. This prevents distortion of the seam and pieces. Then trim off the excess fabric.

Sewing on the Diagonal Using a Square and a Rectangle

Step One: On the wrong side of the fabric, draw a diagonal line across the square. With right sides together, place the square on the rectangle. Stitch a thread or two to the right of the pencil line.

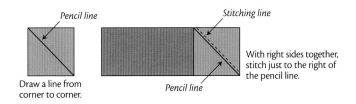

Pencil line

Stitching line

With right sides together, stitch just to the right of the pencil line.

Draw a line from corner to corner.

Pencil line

Step Two: Press the square according to the pressing arrows in the block instructions. Carefully lay the pieces on a cutting mat. Using a ruler and rotary cutter, trim ¼" from the stitching line. You will have a triangle-shaped piece of fabric left over. Discard or save these pieces for future projects. I believe the amount of fabric discarded is well worth the precision and accuracy you gain by using this sewing method.

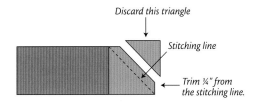

Discard this triangle

Stitching line

Trim ¼" from the stitching line.

Sewing on the Diagonal Using Two Rectangles

In order to draw a pencil line on a rectangle, I position the top rectangle a little away from the edge of the rectangle that is beneath it. Then I can see where to draw my diagonal pencil line. Draw a pencil line from the upper corner diagonally to where the rectangles meet (45°).

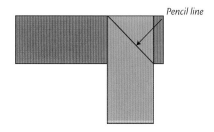

Pencil line

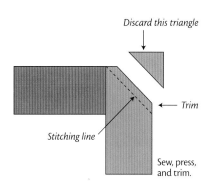

Discard this triangle

Stitching line

Trim

Sew, press, and trim.

Then, I move the top rectangle so the edges of the two rectangles are even. Now I'm ready to sew, press, and trim as instructed above.

PRESSING HINTS

1 Be sure to press each seam allowance before continuing to sew more pieces to the unit.

2 I've included pressing arrows with the block instructions. These are only suggestions but are highly recommended. If you follow these pressing arrows, you should be able to butt most of your pieces together, which will enable you to accurately align and stitch the pieces together. This will keep your blocks square.

3 Do not press using steam. It tends to distort many of the small pieces.

4 Use the cotton setting on your iron. If this doesn't seem hot enough, set it one notch higher. After pressing a piece, it should lie fairly flat on the ironing board. If it doesn't, it's a sure sign that the iron isn't hot enough.

5 To get stubborn seam allowances to lie flat, place a tiny piece of ¼"-wide Steam-a-Seam 2® under the seam allowance and press. This will fuse the seam allowance in place.

EMBELLISHMENT

You may want to embellish your blocks as I did, so I've given you template patterns for some of them. The patterns given are sized for the 12" block. Enlarge or reduce to fit the size of your block. Let your creativity guide you in creating your own embellishments too. The embellishment details should be added after sewing the block. I used a fusible product called Steam-a-Seam 2® by The Warm Company. If you want to appliqué your pieces instead, trace ⅛" from the outside edge of the template. Then turn the edge under ⅛" and hand stitch the pieces in place.

The embellishment options for these blocks are endless. You can personalize them with lettering, add embroidery, sequins, beads, ribbon, trims, jewelry pieces, and much more.

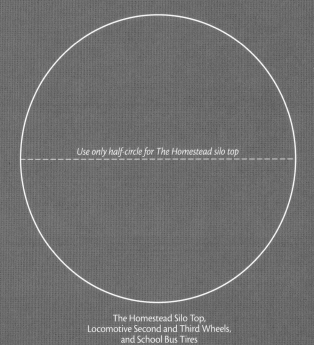

Snow Family Eyes

Snow Family Mouth

Locomotive First Wheel and Birdhouse Hole

School Bus Hub Caps

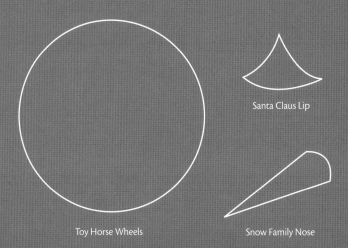

Toy Horse Wheels

Santa Claus Lip

Snow Family Nose

Use only half-circle for The Homestead silo top

The Homestead Silo Top, Locomotive Second and Third Wheels, and School Bus Tires

Hip Hop the Bunny Eye, Fuzzy the Bear Eyes, Freddy the Frog Eyes, Santa Eyes, and Rainbow Fish Eye

Fuzzy the Bear Nose

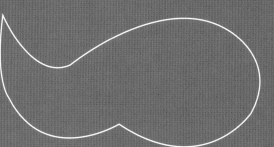

Santa Claus Mustache, reverse for other side

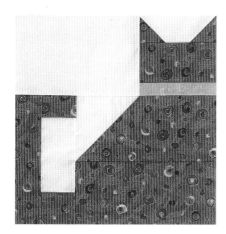

COOL CAT
(Design by Nancy Johnson-Srebro)

You don't have to be a child to love this cat pattern.
Here's a chance to use fun, funky fabrics.

USED FOR	SHAPE/ COLOR	NUMBER TO CUT	BLOCK SIZE			
			6"	8"	10"	12"
A		2	1¼	1½	1¾	2
B		1	1½ X 2½	2 X 3½	2⅜ X 4⅛	2¾ X 5
C		2	2½ X 4½	3 X 6	3⅝ X 7¼	4¼ X 8¾
D		1	1½	1¾	2¼	2½
E		1	1½ X 4½	1¾ X 5½	2 X 6¾	2¼ X 8
F		1	1¼ X 1½	1⅜ X 1¾	1½ X 2¼	1¾ X 2½
G		1	1¼ X 2½	1½ X 3½	1¾ X 4⅛	2 X 5
H		1	2½	3	3⅝	4¼
I		1	1½ X 2¾	1¾ X 3⅜	2¼ X 4	2½ X 4¾
J		1	2½ X 4½	3½ X 5½	4¼ X 6⅞	5 X 8
K		1	¾ X 2½	1 X 3½	1⅛ X 4⅛	1¼ X 5

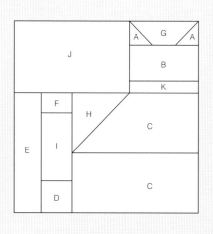

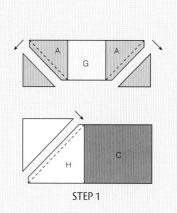

STEP 1

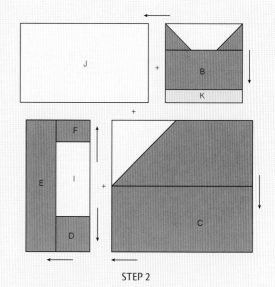

STEP 2

TULIPS GALORE

(Design by Nancy Johnson-Srebro)

These flowers usher in springtime and add beauty and grace to Easter.

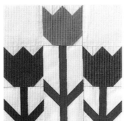

USED FOR	SHAPE/ COLOR	NUMBER TO CUT	BLOCK SIZE			
			6"	9"	12"	15"
A		2	2½	3½	4½	5½
B		18	1	1¼	1½	1¾
C		4	1⅜ X 2	1¾ X 2¾	2⅛ X 3⅜	2½ X 4⅛
D		4	1⅜	1¾	2⅛	2½
E		2	1⅜ X 3	1¾ X 4¼	2⅛ X 5⅜	2½ X 6⅞
F		2	1⅜ X 2⅜	1¾ X 3¼	2⅛ X 4⅛	2½ X 4¾
G		1*	1½ X 2½	2 X 3½	2½ X 4½	3 X 5½
H		2*	1 X 2½	1¼ X 3½	1½ X 4½	1¾ X 5½
I		1*	¾ X 2½	1 X 3½	1¼ X 4½	1½ X 5½
J		2*	1⅜ X 1⅞	1¾ X 2½	2⅛ X 3¼	2½ X 3⅞
K		1	¾ X 4½	1 X 6½	1¼ X 8½	1½ X 10½

*Using different colors, repeat for the other two tulips, stems and leaves.

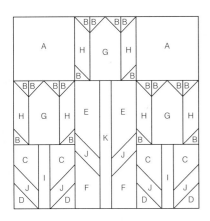

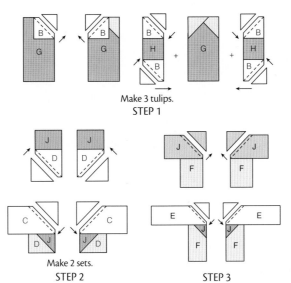

Make 3 tulips.
STEP 1

Make 2 sets.
STEP 2

STEP 3

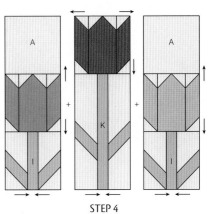

STEP 4

BALLERINA

(Design by Karen F. Srebro)

Watch this ballerina dance when you sew her outfit in lively colors.

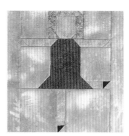

USED FOR	SHAPE/ COLOR	NUMBER TO CUT	BLOCK SIZE			
			6"	9"	12"	15"
A		2	1¼ x 6½	1⅝ x 9½	2 x 12½	2½ x 15½
B		6	⅞	1⅛	1¼	1½
C		2	1⅞ x 2	2½ x 2¾	3¼ x 3½	3¾ x 4¼
D		1	2 x 2½	2¾ x 3½	3½ x 4½	4⅛ x 5½
E		1	2 x 2⅛	2¾ x 2⅞	3½ x 3¾	4⅛ x 4½
F		1	2⅜ x 2⅝	3¼ x 3⅝	4¼ x 4¾	5⅛ x 5¾
G		1	2⅝ x 2¾	3⅝ x 3⅞	4¾ x 5	5¾ x 5⅞
H		1	⅞ x 2¼	1⅛ x 3¼	1¼ x 4	1½ x 5
I		2	⅞ x 1⅝	1⅛ x 2⅛	1¼ x 2¾	1½ x 3¼
J		2	¾	⅞	1	1⅛
K		1	1½ x 1⅝	2 x 2⅛	2½ x 2¾	3 x 3¼
L		2	⅞ x 2⅜	1⅛ x 3⅜	1¼ x 4¼	1½ x 5⅛
M		1	⅞ x 2¼	1⅛ x 3	1¼ x 4	1½ x 4¾
N		1	⅞ x 1⅝	1⅛ x 2⅛	1¼ x 2¾	1½ x 3⅛
O		2	⅞	1⅛	1¼	1½
P		1	2 x 2½	2¾ x 3½	3½ x 4½	4¼ x 5½
Q		2	1⅛	1½	1¾	2
R		1	⅞ x 2	1⅛ x 2¾	1¼ x 3½	1½ x 4¼

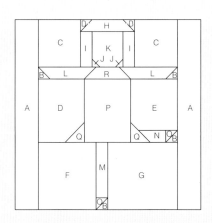

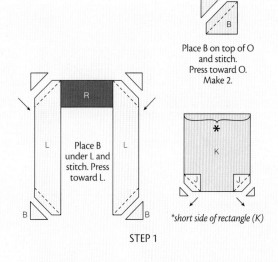

Place B on top of O
and stitch.
Press toward O.
Make 2.

Place B
under L and
stitch. Press
toward L.

*short side of rectangle (K)

STEP 1

Stitch leg unit
to E. Add Q.

STEP 2
*short side of rectangle (E)

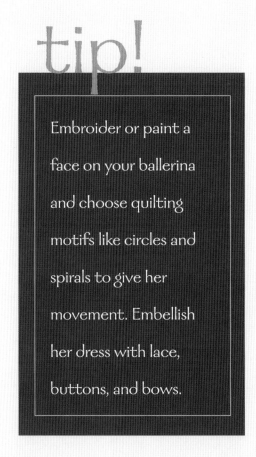

tip!

Embroider or paint a
face on your ballerina
and choose quilting
motifs like circles and
spirals to give her
movement. Embellish
her dress with lace,
buttons, and bows.

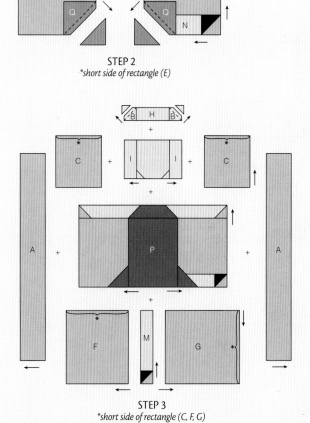

STEP 3
*short side of rectangle (C, F, G)

SCHOOLHOUSE
(Design by Erena Rieflin)

Embellish this schoolhouse with a bell in the tower and a clock over the door.

USED FOR	SHAPE/ COLOR	NUMBER TO CUT	BLOCK SIZE			
			6"	9"	12"	15"
A		4	1¼ x 3	1⅝ x 4¼	2 x 5½	2⅜ x 6¾
B		4	1⅛ x 2	1½ x 2¾	1¾ x 3½	2 x 4¼
C		1	1½	2	2½	3
D		2	¾ x 1¼	⅞ x 1¾	1 x 2	1⅛ x 2½
E		1	2 x 6½	2⅝ x 9½	3½ x 12½	4⅛ x 15½
F		1	1¼ x 2	1⅝ x 2¾	2 x 3½	2⅜ x 4¼
G		2	2	2⅝	3½	4⅛
H		2	1¼ x 2⅞	1¾ x 4	2 x 5¼	2½ x 6⅜
I		2	1¼ x 3½	1⅝ x 5	2 x 6½	2⅜ x 8
J		1	1¼	1¾	2	2½
K		2	1¾ x 2	2¼ x 2¾	3 x 3½	3¾ x 4¼
L		1	1½ x 2½	2 x 3½	2½ x 4½	3 x 5½

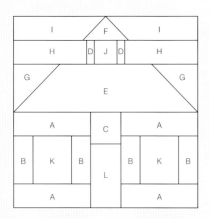

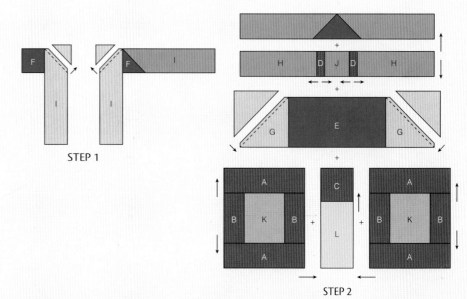

STEP 1

STEP 2

SNOW FAMILY

(Design by Nancy Johnson-Srebro)

Fast and fun —sew and embellish all four sizes to make a snow family!

USED FOR	SHAPE/ COLOR	NUMBER TO CUT	BLOCK SIZE			
			6"	8"	10"	12"
A	▢	1	3¼ x 3¾	3¾ x 4½	4½ x 5½	5½ x 6½
B	◠	1	2 x 2¾	2½ x 3½	3 x 4	3½ x 5
C	▭	1	1½ x 1¾	2 x 2½	2½ x 2½	3 x 3½
D	▬	1	1¼ x 2¾	1¾ x 3½	2 x 4	2 x 5
E	▬	2	1 x 1½	1 x 2	1¼ x 2½	1¼ x 3
F	◣	6	1	1	1¼	1¼
G	▬	2	1⅞ x 3¼	2½ x 3¾	3 x 4½	3½ x 5½
H	▬	2	2⅜ x 3¾	3 x 5¼	3¾ x 6½	4¼ x 7½
Hat	▭	1*	¾ x 1	1¼ x 1½	1¼ x 1½	1¾ x 2½
Hat Brim	▭	1*	¼ x 2	⅜ x 2¾	⅜ x 3½	½ x 4
Scarf	▭	3*	¼ x 1½	¼ x 2¼	⅜ x 2¼	½ x 3¼
Eyes, Nose and Mouth	● ● ◿	2*, 1*, 3*	See page 11			

*Fuse on after sewing the complete block.

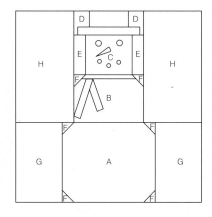

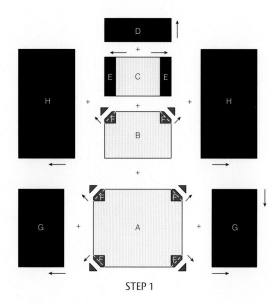

STEP 1

SEWING MACHINE

(Design by Ruth A. Lindhagen)

A good machine is like a trusted friend. It doesn't matter
if it's old or new—it's always there for you!

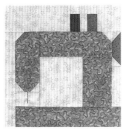

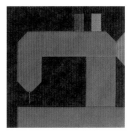

USED FOR	SHAPE/ COLOR	NUMBER TO CUT	BLOCK SIZE			
			6"	8"	10"	12"
A	▭	1	1 x 5¼	1⅛ x 6⅞	1⅜ x 8½	1½ x 10
B	▭	1	1¾ x 3⅞	2⅛ x 5⅛	2½ x 6⅛	3 x 7¼
C	�￀	6	1	1⅛	1⅜	1½
D	▭	2	⅞ x 1	1 x 1⅛	1⅛ x 1⅜	1¼ x 1½
E	▭	1	⅞ x 1¾	1 x 2⅛	1⅛ x 2½	1¼ x 3
F	▭	1	1¾	2⅛	2½	3
G	▭	1	1 x 2½	1⅛ x 3¼	1⅜ x 4	1½ x 4½
H	▭	1	2¾ x 3	3⅝ x 3⅞	4¼ x 4⅞	5 x 5½
I	▭	1	1¼ x 1¾	1½ x 2⅛	1¾ x 2½	2 x 3
J	▽	1	1 x 2¼	1⅛ x 2¾	1⅜ x 3⅜	1½ x 4
K	⬠	1	1¾ x 3½	2⅛ x 4½	2½ x 5⅝	3 x 6½
L	⬟	1	1¾ x 4¼	2⅛ x 5⅝	2½ x 6¾	3 x 8
M	▭	1	2 x 3	2½ x 3⅞	3 x 4⅞	3½ x 5½
N	▭	1	1½ x 6	1⅞ x 7⅞	2⅛ x 9⅝	2½ x 11½
O	▭	2	1 x 1⅜	1⅛ x 1⅝	1⅜ x 1⅞	1½ x 2¼

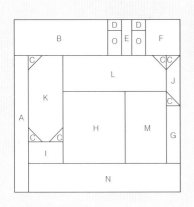

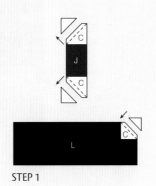

STEP 1

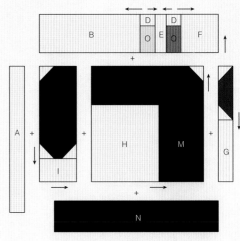

STEP 2

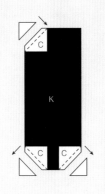

SCAREDY-CAT

(Design by Karen F. Srebro)

Add a moon and small stars in the sky. This cat makes any Halloween setting more exciting.

USED FOR	SHAPE/ COLOR	NUMBER TO CUT	BLOCK SIZE			
			6"	9"	12"	15"
A		20	1	1¼	1½	1¾
B		8	¾ X 1⅛	⅞ X 1½	1 X 1¾	1⅛ X 2⅛
C		2	1⅝ X 3¼	2¼ X 4½	2¾ X 6	3¼ X 7¼
D		1	1½ X 1¾	2 X 2¼	2½ X 3	3 X 3¾
E		2	1⅛ X 2¼	1½ X 3⅛	1¾ X 4	2 X 4⅞
F		1	2¼ X 3¼	3⅛ X 4½	4 X 6	4⅞ X 7¼
G		1	1 X 2	1¼ X 2¾	1½ X 3½	1¾ X 4½
H		1	1 X 1½	1¼ X 2	1½ X 2½	1¾ X 3
I		3	1	1¼	1½	1¾
J		1	1¾ X 2	2⅜ X 2¾	3 X 3½	3⅝ X 4½
K		1	1 X 2¼	1¼ X 3⅛	1½ X 4	1¾ X 4⅞
L		1	2¼ X 4¼	3 X 6	4 X 8	4¾ X 10
M		4	1 X 1½	1¼ X 2	1½ X 2½	1¾ X 3
N		5	1½ X 2	2 X 2⅞	2½ X 3½	3 X 4⅜
O		4	¾	⅞	1	1⅛

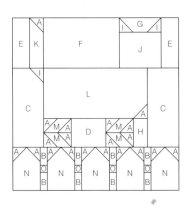

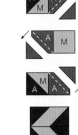

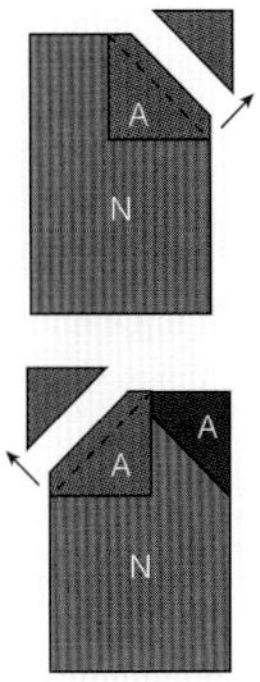

Make 5.
STEP 1

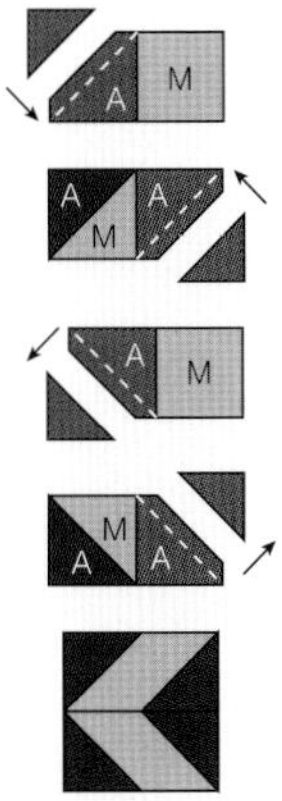

Make 2.
STEP 2

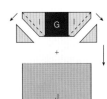

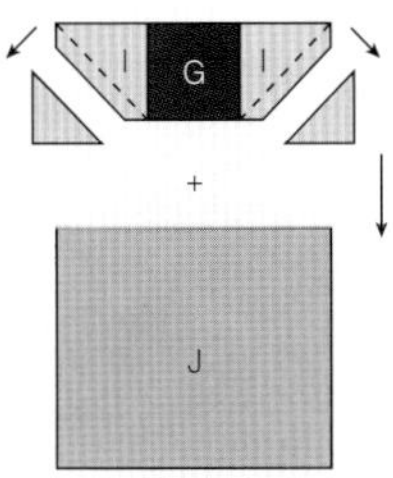

STEP 3

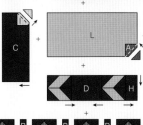

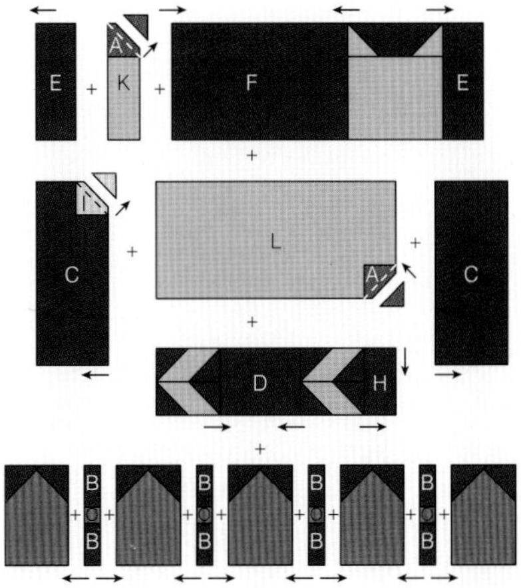

STEP 4

ANGEL OF LOVE

(Design by Cindy Mundy Cochran)

This adorable angel will brighten your life. Embellish her dress with a heart and her head with a halo.

USED FOR	SHAPE/COLOR	NUMBER TO CUT	BLOCK SIZE			
			6"	8"	10"	12"
A		2	1½ x 6½	1⅞ x 8½	2⅛ x 10½	2½ x 12½
B		2	1½ x 2½	1⅞ x 3	2⅛ x 3⅞	2½ x 4½
C		2	1½	1⅞	2⅛	2½
D		2	1	1⅛	1¼	1½
E		2	1½ x 5½	1⅞ x 7⅜	2⅛ x 8¾	2½ x 10½
F		4	1	1⅛	1¼	1½
G		1	1½ x 1⅝	1¾ x 2⅛	2½ x 2⅝	2½ x 2¾
H		2	1 x 1⅝	1⅛ x 2⅛	1¼ x 2⅝	1½ x 2¾
I		1	1 x 2½	1⅛ x 3	1¼ x 4	1½ x 4½
J		1	2½ x 4⅞	3 x 6¼	4 x 7⅝	4½ x 9¼

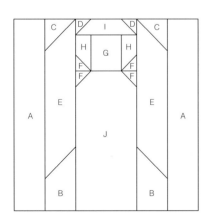

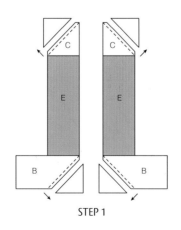

STEP 1

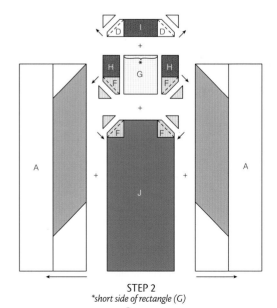

STEP 2

short side of rectangle (G)

PINWHEEL FLOWERS

(Design by Nancy Johnson-Srebro)

With vivid colors, you can make these flowers appear to spin in a soft summer breeze.

USED FOR	SHAPE/ COLOR	NUMBER TO CUT	BLOCK SIZE			
			6"	8"	10"	12"
A	◺	4 ▭	1¾	2⅛	2⅝	3
B	▱	2 ▭	1¾ x 2⅝	2⅛ x 3⅜	2⅝ x 4	3 x 4¾
C	◥	6 ▭	1	1¼	1½	1¾
D	▭	2 ▭	1⅜ x 1¾	1⅝ x 2⅛	2 x 2⅝	2¼ x 3
E	▭	2 ▭	1 x 1¾	1¼ x 2⅛	1¼ x 2⅝	1½ x 3
F	◹	8 ▭	1⅜	1⅝	2	2¼
G	⬭	6 ▭	1¾	2⅛	2⅝	3
H	▭	2 ▭	1 x 3½	1¼ x 4½	1¼ x 5½	1½ x 6½
I	◣	4* ▭	2	2½	3	3½
J	◺	4* ▭	2	2½	3	3½

*Using different colors, repeat for the second flower.

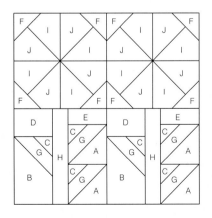

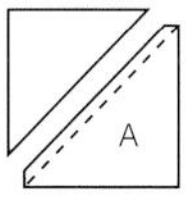

Place A on top of G and stitch. Press toward G. Make 4.

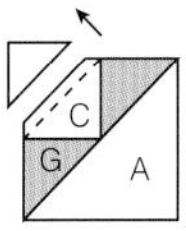

Make 4.
STEP 4

Repeat for the second flower.
STEP 2

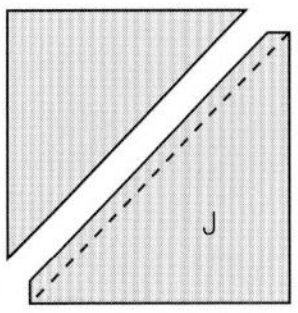

Place J on top of I and stitch. Press toward I. Make 4 sets for each flower.
STEP 1

Make 2.   Make 2.
STEP 3

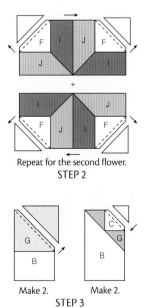

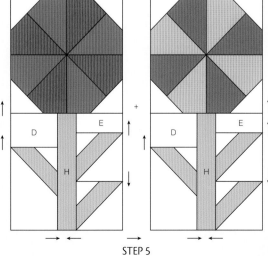

STEP 5

SCHOOL BUS
(Design by Nancy Johnson-Srebro)

What child could resist helping you pick out the fabrics for this special quilt?

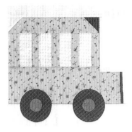

USED FOR	SHAPE/ COLOR	NUMBER TO CUT	BLOCK SIZE			
			6"	9"	12"	15"
A		1	1¾ x 6½	2 x 9½	2¾ x 12½	3½ x 15½
B		1	⅞ x 2	1 x 2¾	1 x 3½	1⅛ x 4¼
C		1	2 x 3	2½ x 4¾	3¼ x 5¾	4 x 7
D		1	1¼	1¾	2	2¼
E		1	1¼ x 6½	1½ x 9½	2 x 12½	2¼ x 15½
F		1	1¼ x 5	1¾ x 7½	2 x 9¾	2¼ x 12
G		1	1 x 2	1½ x 3	1¾ x 3¾	2 x 4½
H		4	⅞ x 2	1⅛ x 3	1¼ x 3¾	1½ x 4½
I		1	2¼ x 5	3¼ x 7½	4 x 9¾	5 x 12
J		1	1⅜ x 2	1¾ x 2¾	2½ x 3½	3 x 4¼
K		1	¾ x 2	¾ x 2¾	¾ x 3½	⅞ x 4¼
L		1	1¼	1¾	2	2¼
M		4	1⅛ x 2	1⅜ x 3	1¾ x 3¾	2 x 4½
Wheels		2*	See page 11			
Hub cap		2*	See page 11			

*Fuse on after sewing the complete block.

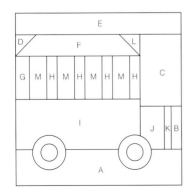
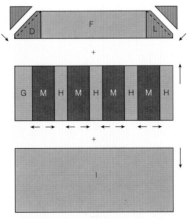
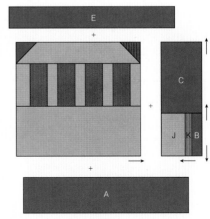

STEP 1

STEP 2

MAX

(Design by Nancy Johnson-Srebro)

For fun, dress this guy in a baseball or football uniform.

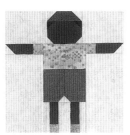 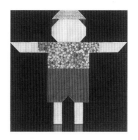 

USED FOR	SHAPE/ COLOR	NUMBER TO CUT	BLOCK SIZE			
			6"	8"	10"	12"
A	▭	2 ▭	2¼ x 4⅜	3 x 5½	3¾ x 6⅞	4⅜ x 8¼
B	◺	4 ☐	⅞	1	1	1⅛
C	▭	2 ☐	2⅛ x 2⅝	2¾ x 3⅜	3¼ x 4	3¾ x 4¾
D	◿	4 ☐	1	1¼	1⅜	1½
E	▭	1 ▭	1¼ x 2	1½ x 2½	1½ x 3	1¾ x 3½
F	▭	2 ▭	⅞ x 2	⅞ x 2½	1 x 3	1⅛ x 3½
G	⬭	1 ☐	1⅝ x 2¼	2 x 2¾	2⅜ x 3½	2¾ x 4
H	⬯	2 ☐	1 x 1¾	1¼ x 2¼	1⅜ x 2⅞	1½ x 3⅜
I	▭	2 ☐	1 x 1½	1⅛ x 1⅞	1¼ x 2¼	1⅜ x 2⅝
J	◻	2 ◻	1	1¼	1⅜	1½
K	▭	1 ▭	1¾ x 3	2⅛ x 3½	2½ x 4	3 x 4¾
L	◤	2 ◼	⅞	1	1	1¼
M	◼◖	2 ▬	1¾ x 2⅛	2 x 2⅝	2¼ x 3¼	2⅝ x 3¾
N	◼	2 ◼	1	1⅛	1¼	1⅜
O	◣	1 ▬	1 x 2¼	1¼ x 2¾	1⅜ x 3½	1½ x 4

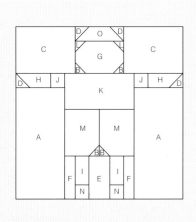

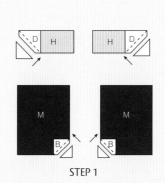

STEP 1

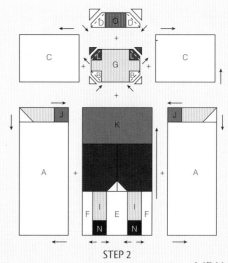

STEP 2

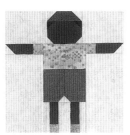 MAX

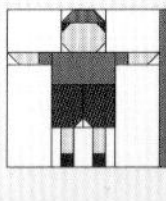

LOCOMOTIVE

(Design by Folker G. Rieflin)

You can make this locomotive look like an antique or toy train. Enjoy the ride!

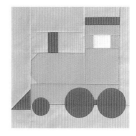

USED FOR	SHAPE/ COLOR	NUMBER TO CUT	BLOCK SIZE			
			6"	8"	10"	12"
A	▭	1 ▭	1⅞ x 3¼	2 x 4	2¾ x 4⅞	3¼ x 6
B	▭	1 ▭	1⅛ x 2¼	1⅛ x 2⅞	1½ x 3½	1¾ x 4
C	▭	1 ▭	1½ x 1⅞	2 x 2¼	2¼ x 2½	2½ x 3¼
D	▭	2 ▭	1⅜ x 1½	1⅝ x 2	2 x 2¼	2¼ x 2½
E	◺	1 ▭	1½ x 5⅝	2 x 7⅜	2¼ x 9	2½ x 10¾
F	◹	2 ▫	⅞	1	1⅛	1¼
G	▭	1 ▭	1 x 5⅜	1⅛ x 7	1⅜ x 8½	1½ x 10¼
H	▭	1 ▭	1⅝ x 5½	2 x 7	2½ x 8¾	2¾ x 10½
I	▭	1 ▭	⅞ x 2¼	1 x 2⅞	1⅛ x 3½	1¼ x 4
J	▭	1 ▭	1 x 1½	1⅛ x 2	1⅜ x 2¼	1½ x 2½
K	◹	1 ▪	1½	2	2¼	2½
L	▭	2 ▭	⅞ x 1⅛	1 x 1⅜	1¼ x 1½	1⅜ x 1¾
M	▪	1 ▪	2¼	2⅞	3½	4
N	▭	1 ▭	2 x 3¼	2½ x 4	3 x 4⅞	3½ x 6
O	▭	1 ▭	1½ x 5	2 x 6⅜	2 x 7⅞	2½ x 9½
P	▭	1 ▭	1 x 2¼	1⅛ x 2⅞	1⅜ x 3½	1½ x 4
Q	▭	1 ▭	1⅛ x 1½	1⅜ x 1⅞	1½ x 2	1¾ x 2¼
Wheels	● ●	1*, 2*	See page 11			

*Fuse on after sewing the complete block.

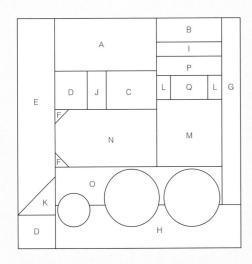

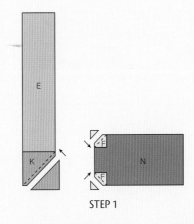

STEP 1

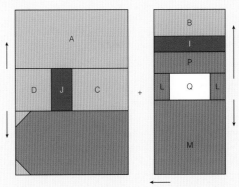

STEP 2

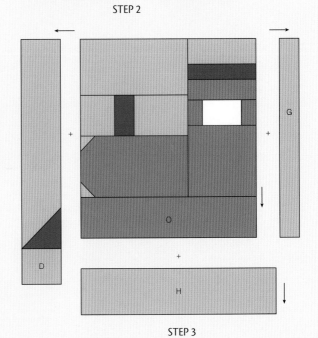

STEP 3

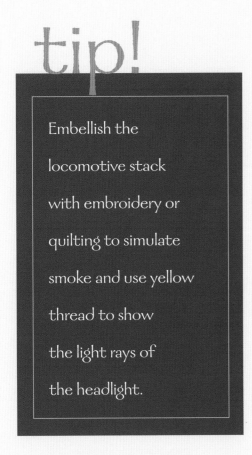

tip!

Embellish the locomotive stack with embroidery or quilting to simulate smoke and use yellow thread to show the light rays of the headlight.

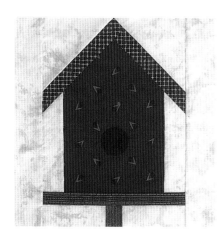

BIRDHOUSE

(Design by Nancy Johnson-Srebro)

To personalize your birdhouse, add flowers, stars, hearts, or birds.

USED FOR	SHAPE/ COLOR	NUMBER TO CUT	BLOCK SIZE			
			6"	8"	10"	12"
A		2	1⅛ x 2⅜	1⅜ x 3⅛	1¾ x 3½	1¾ x 4¼
B		2	1⅜ x 6½	1½ x 8½	2 x 10½	2¼ x 12½
C		2	1⅛ x 4¾	1⅜ x 6¼	1½ x 7⅜	1¾ x 9¼
D		2	2⅝	3½	4	4¾
E		1	2⅝ x 3⅜	3½ x 4⅜	4 x 5¼	4¾ x 6
F		1	3⅜	4⅜	5¼	6
G		1	3½ x 4¾	4¾ x 6¼	5½ x 7⅜	6½ x 9¼
H		1	⅞ x 4¾	1 x 6½	1⅛ x 7½	1¼ x 9
I		1	1 x 1⅛	1¼ x 1⅜	1½ x 1¾	1½ x 1¾
Hole	●	1*	See page 11			

*Fuse on after sewing the complete block.

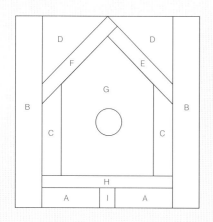

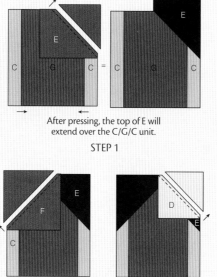

After pressing, the top of E will
extend over the C/G/C unit.

STEP 1

Line up the top of F with the top of E.
Also, line up the edge of F with the edge of C.

STEP 2

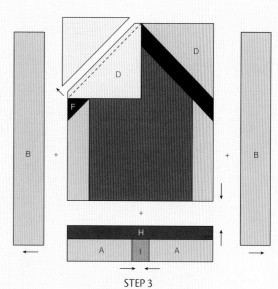

STEP 3

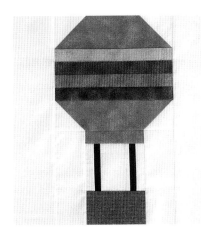

HOT AIR BALLOON

(Design by Cindy Mundy Cochran)

You'll want to make sure you use lots of color for this block as you float through the air.

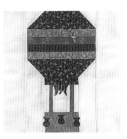

USED FOR	SHAPE/ COLOR	NUMBER TO CUT	BLOCK SIZE			
			6"	9"	12"	15"
A	▭	2 ▭	1¾ x 6½	2⅜ x 9½	3 x 12½	3⅝ x 15½
B	◺	4 ▫	1⅜	1¾	2¼	2½
C	▭	2 ▭	1⅜ x 3¼	1¾ x 4½	2¼ x 6	2½ x 7½
D	▭	2 ▭	¾ x 1⅞	1 x 2⅜	1 x 3¼	1¼ x 4
E	▭	1 ▭	1¼ x 1⅞	1¾ x 2⅜	2¼ x 3¼	2¾ x 4
F	▬	1 ▬	1½ x 2¼	2 x 3¼	2½ x 4	3 x 5¼
G	◹	2 ▬	1⅜ x 4	1¾ x 5¾	2¼ x 7½	2½ x 9¼
H	▬	1 ▬	⅞ x 2¼	1⅛ x 3¼	1¼ x 4	1½ x 5¼
I	▬	1* ▬	⅞ x 4	1⅛ x 5¾	1¼ x 7½	1½ x 9¼
J	▬	2 ▬	¾ x 1⅞	¾ x 2⅜	⅞ x 3¼	1 x 4

* Repeat using four different colors.

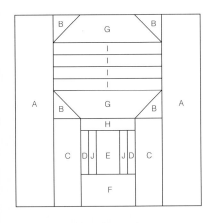

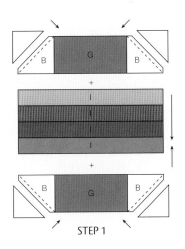

STEP 1

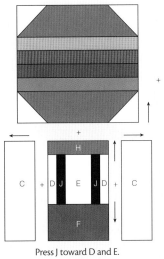

Press J toward D and E.

STEP 2

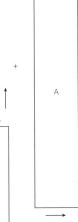

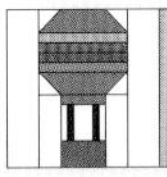

MAGIC WATERING CAN

(Design by Nancy Johnson-Srebro)

You can create the magic of any season by cutting and fusing different flowers to your block. This would make a charming quilt.

USED FOR	SHAPE/ COLOR	NUMBER TO CUT	BLOCK SIZE			
			6"	9"	12"	15"
A		1	3½ x 4½	5 x 6¾	6½ x 8¾	8 x 11
B		1	2½ x 3¼	3¼ x 4½	4¼ x 5¾	5 x 7
C		1	1⅝	2	2⅝	3¼
D		1	2½ x 3¾	3¼ x 5½	4¼ x 7¼	5 x 9
E		3	⅞	1	1¼	1½
F		1	1 x 1¾	1¼ x 3	1½ x 3	1¾ x 3½
G		1	1⅜ x 3½	2 x 5	2½ x 6½	3 x 8
H		2	1 x 1⅜	1 x 1¾	1½ x 2¼	1¾ x 2¾
I		1	2¾ x 3½	4 x 5	5 x 6½	6¼ x 8
J		1	2½	3¼	4¼	5
K		2	⅞ x 1	1 x 1¼	1¼ x 1½	1½ x 1¾
L		1	⅞ x 2½	1 x 4	1¼ x 4½	1½ x 5½
M		1*	½ x 2¾	½ x 4	¾ x 5	¾ x 6¾

*Fuse on after sewing the complete block.

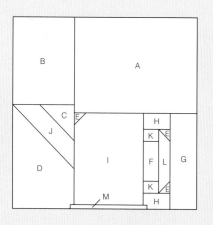

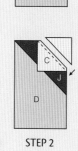

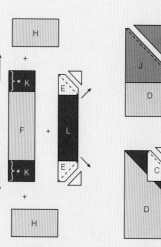

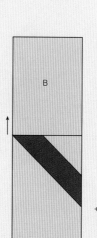

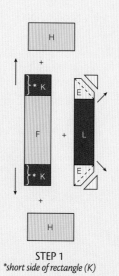

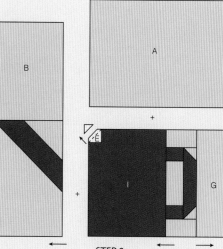

STEP 1
*short side of rectangle (K)

STEP 2

STEP 3

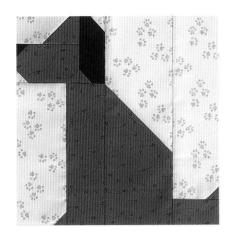

RUFF THE DOG
(Design by Nancy Johnson-Srebro)

Who could resist this adorable dog?
Dress him by fusing a collar or a bandana around his neck.

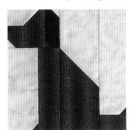  

USED FOR	SHAPE/ COLOR	NUMBER TO CUT	BLOCK SIZE			
			6"	8"	10"	12"
A		1	1¾ X 5¾	2¼ X 7½	2¾ X 9¼	3¼ X 11
B		1	2½ X 4¼	3¼ X 5¾	3¾ X 7	4½ X 8¼
C		1	2 X 4¾	2½ X 6	3 X 7¼	3½ X 8¾
D		2	⅞	1	1⅛	1¼
E		1	1¼ X 2	1½ X 2½	1¾ X 3	2 X 3½
F		1	1¼ X 1⅝	1½ X 2	1¾ X 2½	2 X 2¾
G		1	1½ X 2⅜	2 X 3	2½ X 3¾	2¾ X 4¼
H		3	⅞	1	1⅛	1¼
I		1	1¾ X 4¾	2 X 6	2½ X 7¼	2¾ X 8¾
J		1	2½ X 4¾	3¼ X 6	3¾ X 7¼	4½ X 8¾
K		1	1¼ X 1¾	1½ X 2¼	1¾ X 2¾	2 X 3¼
L		1	1⅜ X 2¼	1½ X 3	1¾ X 3¾	2 X 4¼
M		1	⅞	1	1⅛	1¼

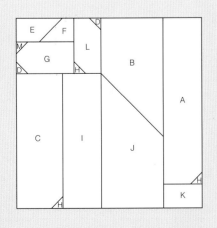

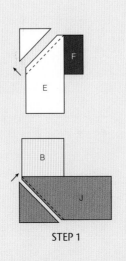

STEP 1

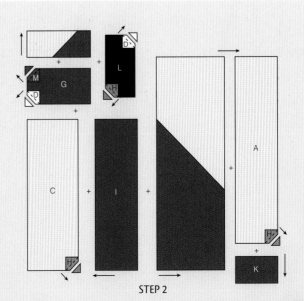

STEP 2

FREDDY THE FROG

(Design by Cindy Mundy Cochran)

Make his body one color and the legs another color.

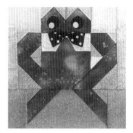

USED FOR	SHAPE/ COLOR	NUMBER TO CUT	BLOCK SIZE			
			6"	8"	10"	12"
A	▭	2 ▭	1 x 4½	1 x 5⅞	1½ x 7⅛	1½ x 8½
B	◸ ▢	4 ▢	1¾	2¼	2½	3
C	◺	6 ▢	1⅛	1⅜	1½	1¾
D	◺	2 ▢	1	1⅛	1⅜	1½
E	◺	2 ▭	1¾ x 2⅛	2¼ x 2⅝	2½ x 3¼	3 x 3¾
F	◣	2 ▪	1¼	1½	1¾	2
G	▬	2 ▪	1½ x 2½	1¾ x 3⅛	2¼ x 3⅞	2½ x 4½
H	⬢	1 ▪	2½ x 4½	3⅛ x 6	3⅞ x 7	4½ x 8½
I	⬭	2 ▢	2¼	2¾	3½	4
J	⬭	2 ▢	2¾	3½	4¼	5
K	⬠	1 ▭	3 x 3¼	4 x 4⅛	4½ x 5⅛	5½ x 6
L	⬠	2 ▭	1⅝ x 1¾	2 x 2¼	2⅜ x 2½	2¾ x 3
M	⬠	2 ▢	1¾	2¼	2½	3
Eyes	●	2*	See page 11			

*Fuse on after sewing the complete block.

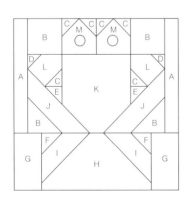

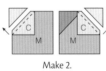

Make 2.

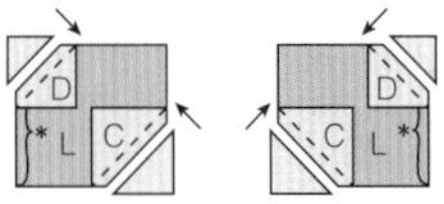

*short side of rectangle (L)

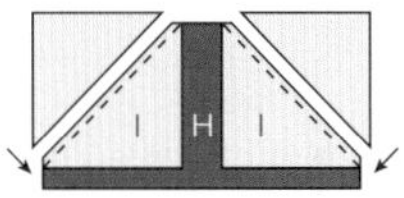

STEP 1

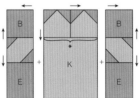

STEP 2
*short side of rectangle (K)

Line up the bottom and side edge of J with E.

STEP 3

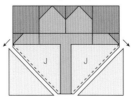

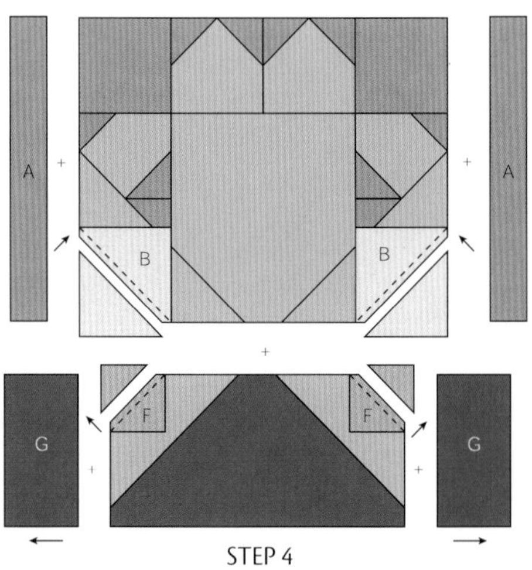

STEP 4

SAMANTHA
(Design by Nancy Johnson-Srebro)

Our granddaughter Casey loves to play with her cousin Sammi.
What fun a child would have naming each girl block after her friends.

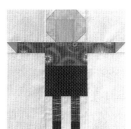  

USED FOR	SHAPE/ COLOR	NUMBER TO CUT	BLOCK SIZE			
			6"	8"	10"	12"
A	▭	2 ▭	2⅜ X 4⅜	3 X 5½	3¾ X 6⅞	4⅜ X 8¼
B	▭	2 ▭	⅞ X 2¼	1 X 2¾	1⅛ X 3½	1¼ X 4
C	▭	2 ▭	2⅛ X 2½	2¾ X 3⅛	3¼ X 3⅞	3¾ X 4½
D	◺	6 ▢	1	1¼	1⅜	1½
E	▭	1 ▭	1 X 2¼	1¼ X 2¾	1¼ X 3½	1½ X 4
F	▲	1 ▮	1 X 2½	1¼ X 3¼	1⅜ X 3¾	1½ X 4½
G	◣◢	2 ▮	1 X 1⅝	1¼ X 2	1⅜ X 2⅜	1½ X 2¾
H	▭	1 ▭	1½ X 1⅝	1¾ X 2	2 X 2⅜	2½ X 2¾
I	◳	2 ▢	1	1¼	1⅜	1½
J	▭	2 ▭	1 X 1⅞	1¼ X 2¼	1⅜ X 2⅞	1½ X 3⅜
K	▭	1 ▭	1⅝ X 2¾	2 X 3½	2¼ X 4	2¾ X 4¾
L	▭	1 ▭	2 X 2¾	2½ X 3½	3 X 4	3½ X 4¾
M	▭	2 ▭	1 X 1¾	1⅛ X 2⅛	1¼ X 2¾	1⅜ X 3⅛
N	■	2 ■	1	1⅛	1¼	1⅜

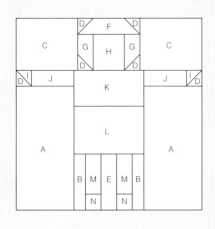

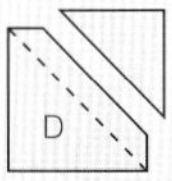

Place D on top of I
and stitch. Press toward I.
Make 2.

STEP 1

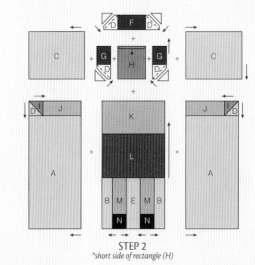

STEP 2
*short side of rectangle (H)

CAMPBELL'S BEACH HOUSE

(Design by Nancy Johnson-Srebro)

When I need some rest and relaxation, I know I can always visit my friends, Bonnie and Arlington Campbell, at their beach house in Virginia.

USED FOR	SHAPE/ COLOR	NUMBER TO CUT	BLOCK SIZE			
			6"	8"	10"	12"
A		2	1 X 2	1⅜ X 2½	1¾ X 3	1¾ X 3½
B		2	1¼ X 1½	1½ X 1¾	1¾ X 2	2¼ X 2½
C		1	1½	1¾	2	2½
D		4	1⅛ X 1½	1¼ X 1¾	1⅜ X 2	1½ X 2½
E		4	1 X 2½	1⅛ X 3¼	1¼ X 4	1⅜ X 4½
F		2	1¼ X 1½	1⅝ X 1¾	2 X 2⅛	2¼ X 2½
G		1	2 X 6½	2½ X 8½	2¾ X 10½	3½ X 12½
H		2	1½ X 1¾	1¾ X 2⅛	2 X 2⅜	2½ X 2¾
I		1	1½ X 6½	1⅝ X 8½	2 X 10½	2¼ X 12½
J		1	1½ X 2½	1¾ X 3¼	2 X 4	2½ X 4½
K		1	4	5⅜	6¾	7¾
L		1	3½ X 4	4½ X 5⅜	5½ X 6¾	6½ X 7¾
M		2	1 X 2	1⅜ X 2½	1¾ X 3	1¾ X 3½
N		2	3½	4½	5½	6½

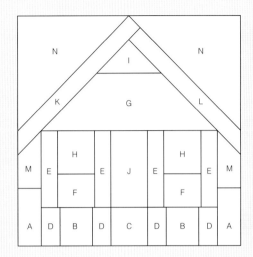

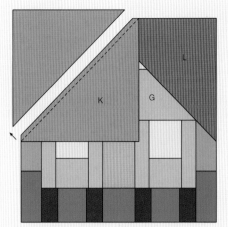

Line up top of K with the top of L.
Also, line up the edge of K with the edge of G/I.
STEP 4

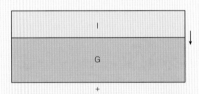

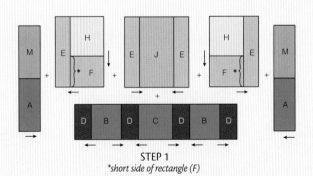

STEP 1
*short side of rectangle (F)

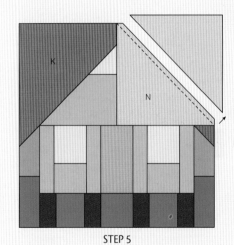

STEP 5

STEP 2

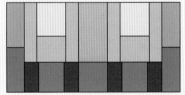

After pressing, the top of L will extend over I.
STEP 3

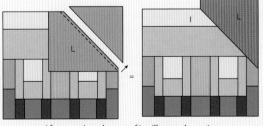

STEP 6

PATCHES THE COW
(Design by Nancy Johnson-Srebro)

Rearrange the patches any way you wish to create a design just for you.

USED FOR	SHAPE/ COLOR	NUMBER TO CUT	BLOCK SIZE			
			6"	8"	10"	12"
A	△	4 ☐	1	$1\frac{1}{8}$	$1\frac{3}{8}$	$1\frac{1}{2}$
B	⬢ ☐	2 ☐	1 x $1\frac{1}{4}$	$1\frac{1}{8}$ x $1\frac{1}{2}$	$1\frac{3}{8}$ x $1\frac{3}{4}$	$1\frac{1}{2}$ x 2
C	☐	1 ☐	$2\frac{1}{8}$ x $4\frac{3}{4}$	$2\frac{3}{4}$ x $6\frac{1}{4}$	$3\frac{1}{4}$ x $7\frac{1}{2}$	$3\frac{3}{4}$ x 9
D	☐	1 ☐	$1\frac{3}{4}$ x $2\frac{3}{4}$	$2\frac{1}{8}$ x $3\frac{1}{2}$	$2\frac{5}{8}$ x $4\frac{1}{4}$	3 x 5
E	☐	2 ☐	$1\frac{7}{8}$ x $2\frac{1}{4}$	$2\frac{1}{4}$ x $2\frac{3}{4}$	$2\frac{3}{4}$ x $3\frac{1}{2}$	$3\frac{1}{4}$ x 4
F	☐	1 ☐	$1\frac{7}{8}$ x 2	$2\frac{1}{4}$ x $2\frac{1}{2}$	$2\frac{3}{4}$ x 3	$3\frac{1}{4}$ x $3\frac{1}{2}$
G	⬡	1 ☐	$1\frac{1}{2}$ x $2\frac{7}{8}$	$1\frac{7}{8}$ x $3\frac{7}{8}$	$2\frac{1}{8}$ x $4\frac{5}{8}$	$2\frac{1}{2}$ x $5\frac{1}{2}$
H	◺	1 ☐	$1\frac{1}{2}$	$1\frac{7}{8}$	$2\frac{1}{8}$	$2\frac{1}{2}$
I	▮ ▰	10* ▮	$1\frac{1}{4}$	$1\frac{1}{2}$	$1\frac{3}{4}$	2
J	▬	1 ▬	$1\frac{5}{8}$ x $2\frac{1}{4}$	$2\frac{1}{8}$ x $2\frac{3}{4}$	$2\frac{3}{8}$ x $3\frac{1}{2}$	$2\frac{3}{4}$ x 4
K	◣	4 ▮	1	$1\frac{1}{8}$	$1\frac{3}{8}$	$1\frac{1}{2}$
L	▮	1 ▮	$1\frac{1}{4}$	$1\frac{1}{2}$	$1\frac{3}{4}$	2
M	▬	2 ▬	1 x $1\frac{7}{8}$	$1\frac{1}{4}$ x $2\frac{1}{4}$	$1\frac{1}{4}$ x $2\frac{3}{4}$	$1\frac{1}{2}$ x $3\frac{1}{4}$
N	▱	1 ▬	$1\frac{1}{2}$ x $2\frac{1}{8}$	$1\frac{7}{8}$ x $2\frac{1}{2}$	$2\frac{1}{8}$ x 3	$2\frac{1}{2}$ x $3\frac{1}{2}$

*Repeat using a different color.

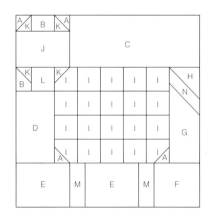

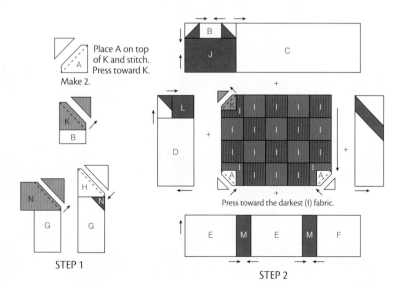

Place A on top of K and stitch. Press toward K. Make 2.

Press toward the darkest (I) fabric.

STEP 1

STEP 2

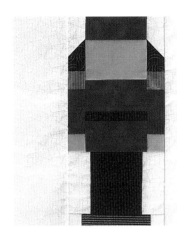

NUTCRACKER
(Design by Cindy Mundy Cochran)

Incorporate this fellow into a Christmas wallhanging or a pillow for holiday cheer.

USED FOR	SHAPE/ COLOR	NUMBER TO CUT	BLOCK SIZE			
			6"	9"	12"	15"
A		2	2 x 6½	2⅞ x 9½	3¾ x 12½	4½ x 15½
B		2	1 x 1¾	1¼ x 2⅜	1½ x 3	1¾ x 3⅝
C		2	1¼ x 2¼	1½ x 3⅛	1¾ x 4	2⅛ x 4⅞
D		2	⅞	1	1¼	1½
E		1	1¼ x 2½	1⅝ x 3¼	2 x 4	2⅜ x 5
F		2	1 x 1¾	1¼ x 2⅜	1½ x 3	1¾ x 3⅝
G		2	1⅜ x 2½	1⅞ x 3¼	2¼ x 4	2⅝ x 5
H		1	¾ x 2½	⅞ x 3¼	1 x 4	1⅛ x 5
I		2	1¼ x 2¼	1⅝ x 3⅛	2 x 4	2⅜ x 4⅞
J		2	1	1¼	1½	1¾
K		1	1⅝ x 2½	2⅛ x 3¼	2¾ x 4	3⅜ x 5
L		2	1 x 1⅜	1¼ x 1⅞	1½ x 2¼	1¾ x 2⅝
M		2	1	1¼	1½	1¾
N		1	⅞ x 2¾	1 x 3¾	1¼ x 4½	1½ x 5½

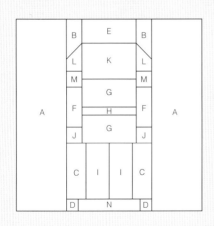

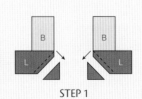

STEP 1

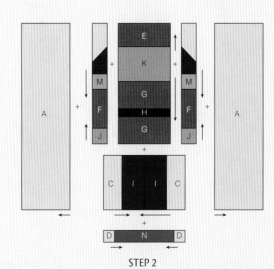

STEP 2

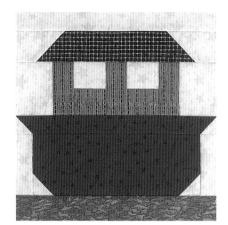

NOAH'S ARK

(Design by Nancy Johnson-Srebro)

You could easily embellish the ark with animals in the windows.
How about some small and large waves splashing on the boat?

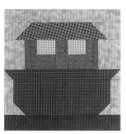

USED FOR	SHAPE/ COLOR	NUMBER TO CUT	BLOCK SIZE			
			6"	8"	10"	12"
A		1	1¼ x 6½	1½ x 8½	1¾ x 10½	2 x 12½
B		2	1 x 2¼	1¼ x 3	1⅜ x 3½	1½ x 4
C		2	1⅛	1⅜	1½	1¾
D		2	1	1¼	1⅜	1½
E		2	1¾ x 2	2⅛ x 2½	2⅜ x 3	2¾ x 3½
F		2	1⅜ x 2⅛	1⅜ x 2¼	2 x 3	2¼ x 3½
G		1	1⅛ x 6½	1⅜ x 8½	1⅜ x 10½	1¾ x 12½
H		1	1⅜ x 5	1⅜ x 6¾	2 x 8½	2¼ x 10
I		3	1 x 2	1¼ x 2½	1½ x 3	1¾ x 3½
J		2	1¼ x 1½	1½ x 1¾	1¾ x 2⅛	2 x 2⅜
K		2	1¼ x 1½	1½ x 1¾	1¾ x 2⅛	2 x 2⅜
L		1	1 x 6½	1¼ x 8½	1⅜ x 10½	1½ x 12½
M		1	2¼ x 5½	3 x 7	3½ x 8¾	4 x 10½

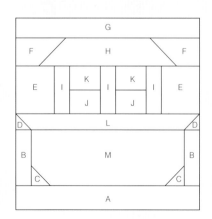

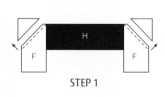

STEP 1

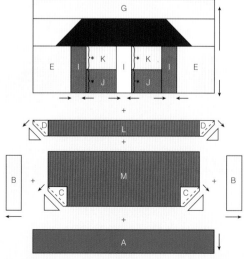

STEP 2
*short side of rectangle (J,K)

TOY HORSE

(Design by Nancy Johnson-Srebro)

How many of you remember growing up with this toy?

USED FOR	SHAPE/ COLOR	NUMBER TO CUT	BLOCK SIZE			
			6"	8"	10"	12"
A	▭	1 ▭	1½ x 6½	1¾ x 8½	2 x 10½	2¼ x 12½
B	▭	2 ▭	1¼ x 5½	1½ x 7¼	1¾ x 9	2 x 10¾
C	▭	2 ▭	1⅜ x 3⅛	1⅝ x 4⅛	2 x 5	2¼ x 6
D	▭	1 ▭	1½ x 1⅝	2 x 2⅛	2¼ x 2½	2½ x 2¾
E	▱	1 ▭	2¼ x 3¼	2¾ x 4¼	3½ x 5	4 x 6
F	◺	2 ▢	1⅜	1⅝	2	2¼
G	◺	1 ▢	¾	⅞	1	1
H	⬠	1 ▪	2¼	2¾	3½	4
I	▭	1 ▭	2 x 3¼	2½ x 4¼	3 x 5	3¾ x 6
J	▭	2 ▭	1⅜ x 1⅝	1⅝ x 2⅛	1⅞ x 2½	2¼ x 2¾
K	◣	1 ▪	1⅜	1⅝	2	2¼
L	▭	1 ▭	1⅛ x 5	1⅜ x 6½	1½ x 8	1¾ x 9½
Wheels	●	2*	See page 11			

*Fuse on after sewing the complete block.

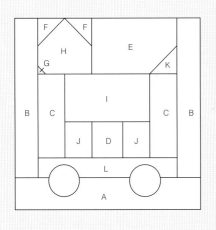

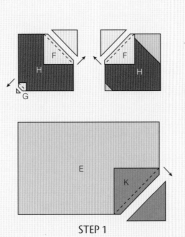

STEP 1

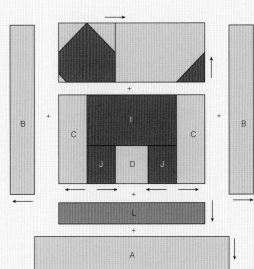

STEP 2

THE HOMESTEAD
(Design by Erena Rieflin)

Accent this block with animals, flowers, hay, vines, and cornstalks as embellishments.

  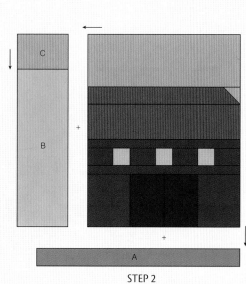

USED FOR	SHAPE/ COLOR	NUMBER TO CUT	BLOCK SIZE			
			6"	9"	12"	15"
A		1	1 x 6½	1¼ x 9½	1½ x 12½	1¾ x 15½
B		1	2 x 5	2¾ x 7¼	3½ x 9½	4¼ x 11¾
C		1	1½ x 2	2 x 2¾	2½ x 3½	3 x 4¼
D		1	2 x 5	2¾ x 7¼	3½ x 9½	4¼ x 11¾
E		1	1	1¼	1½	1¾
F		1	1 X 5	1¼ x 7¼	1½ x 9½	1¾ x 11¾
G		1	1½ x 5	2 x 7¼	2½ x 9½	3 x 11¾
H		2	¾ x 5	⅞ x 7¼	1 x 9½	1⅛ x 11¾
I		4	1 x 1¼	1¼ x 1⅝	1½ x 2	1¾ x 2⅜
J		2	1¾ x 2	2⅜ x 2¾	3 x 3½	3⅝ x 4¼
K		3	1	1¼	1½	1¾
L		2	1½ x 2	2 x 2¾	2½ x 3½	3 x 4¼
Top of Silo		1*	See page 11			

* Fuse on after sewing the complete block

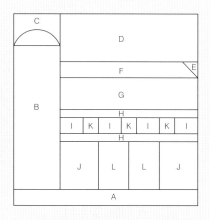

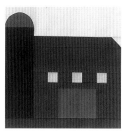

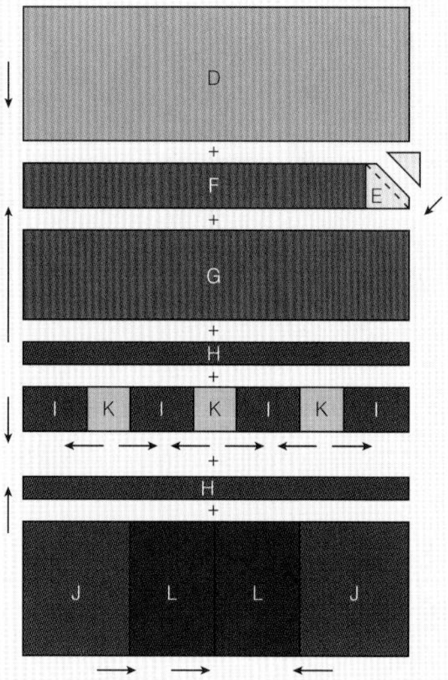

STEP 1

STEP 2

COUNTRY COTTAGE

(Design by Nancy Johnson-Srebro)

This little cottage is a great summer getaway.
There are endless ways to decorate it.

USED FOR	SHAPE/ COLOR	NUMBER TO CUT	BLOCK SIZE			
			6"	8"	10"	12"
A	▬	1 ▬	1 x 2½	1¼ x 3¼	1½ x 3¾	1½ x 4½
B	▬	1 ▬	1½ x 4	2 x 5	2¼ x 6	2½ x 7½
C	▬	2 ▬	1⅛ x 1½	1¼ x 1¾	1½ x 2	1¾ x 2½
D	▬	1 ▬	1½ x 5½	2 x 7	2¼ x 8½	2½ x 10½
E	▬	2 ▬	⅞ x 1½	1 x 1¾	1⅛ x 2	1¼ x 2½
F	▬	1 ▬	1½ x 2	1¾ x 2½	2 x 2¾	2½ x 3½
G	▬	1 ▬	1½ x 2½	1¾ x 3¼	2 x 3¾	2½ x 4½
H	◢◣	1 ▬	2 x 6½	2½ x 8½	3 x 10½	3½ x 12½
I	▬	1 ▬	1½ x 1¾	1½ x 2¼	2 x 2½	2½ x 3
J	▭	2 ▭	1½ x 2⅞	1½ x 3⅝	2 x 4½	2½ x 5¼
K	◺	2 ▭	2	2½	3	3½
L	▭	2 ▭	1 x 3½	1¼ x 4¾	1½ x 5½	1½ x 6½
M	▬	1 ▬	1 x 6½	1¼ x 8½	1½ x 10½	1½ x 12½

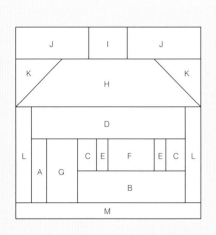

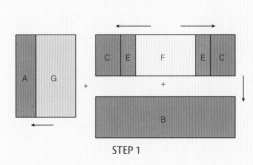

STEP 1

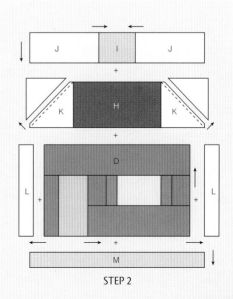

STEP 2

PENNY THE HEN
(Design by Cindy Mundy Cochran)

Every barnyard needs a flock of hens.

 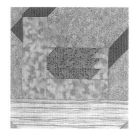 

USED FOR	SHAPE/ COLOR	NUMBER TO CUT	BLOCK SIZE			
			6"	8"	10"	12"
A		1	1⅛ x 1⅝	1⅜ x 2	1½ x 2⅜	1¾ x 2¾
B		1	1⅛ x 3⅞	1⅜ x 5	1½ x 6⅛	1¾ x 7¼
C		4	1	1⅛	1⅜	1½
D		1	2½ x 4⅝	3¼ x 6	3¾ x 7½	4½ x 8¾
E		1	1½ x 3	1¾ x 3¾	2¼ x 4¾	2½ x 5½
F		1	⅞	1	1⅛	1¼
G		1	1	1⅛	1⅜	1½
H		1	1 x 1¾	1⅛ x 2⅛	1⅜ x 2½	1½ x 3
I		2	1½	1¾	2¼	2½
J		2	1⅛	1⅜	1½	1¾
K		1	1¾ x 4½	2⅛ x 5⅞	2½ x 7⅛	3 x 8½
L		3	1	1⅛	1⅜	1½
M		1	1½ x 3⅝	1⅞ x 4¾	2⅛ x 5¾	2½ x 6¾
N		3	1 x 1⅜	1⅛ x 1⅝	1⅜ x 2	1½ x 2¼
O		3	1 x 3¼	1⅛ x 4¼	1⅜ x 5⅛	1½ x 6
P		1	2 x 6½	2½ x 8½	3 x 10½	3½ x 12½

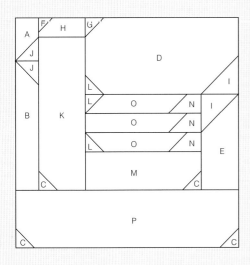

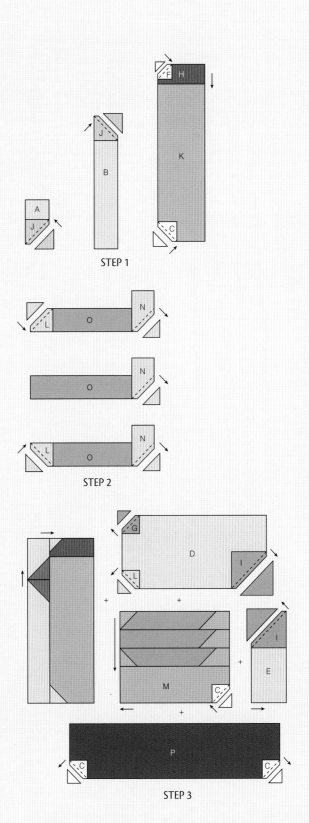

STEP 1

STEP 2

STEP 3

TOWN HOUSES

(Design by Nancy Johnson-Srebro)

Wouldn't a row of town houses make a wonderful border for a quilt?

USED FOR	SHAPE/ COLOR	NUMBER TO CUT	BLOCK SIZE			
			6"	9"	12"	15"
A		1	1⅛ x 6½	1½ x 9½	1¾ x 12½	2 x 15½
B		2*	1 x 4⅜	1¼ x 6¼	1½ x 8¼	1¾ x 10¼
C		1*	1¼ x 1½	1½ x 2	2 x 2½	2⅜ x 3
D		3	¾ x 1½	⅞ x 2	1 x 2½	1⅛ x 3
E		1*	1½ x 2¼	2 x 3⅛	2½ x 4	3 x 4⅞
F		1*	1½ x 1⅝	2 x 2¼	2½ x 2¾	3 x 3⅜
G		1*	2 x 2½	2¾ x 3½	3½ x 4½	4¼ x 5½
H		6	1½	2	2½	3

*Using different colors, repeat the cutting for the other houses.

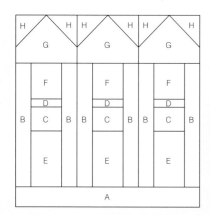

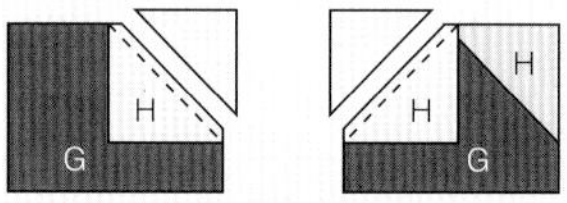

Make 3 roofs using different colors.
Press toward H on the first and last roofs.
Press toward G on the middle roof.

STEP 1

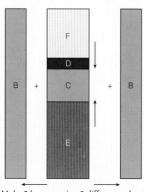

Make 3 houses using 3 different colors.

STEP 2

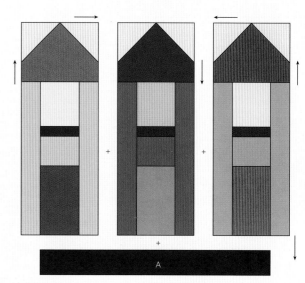

STEP 3

MY HEART BELONGS TO THE STARS

(Design by Karen F. Srebro)

Dig into your stash of fabrics and start cutting!
The secret to this block is in the pressing.

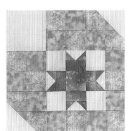

USED FOR	SHAPE/ COLOR	NUMBER TO CUT	BLOCK SIZE 6"	9"	12"	15"
A		1	2½	3½	4½	5½
B		2	2	2¾	3½	4¼
C		4	1½	2	2½	3
D		4	1 X 1½	1¼ X 2	1½ X 2½	1¾ X 3
E		8	1	1¼	1½	1¾
F		4	1 X 1½	1¼ X 2	1½ X 2½	1¾ X 3
G		1	1½	2	2½	3
H		23*	1½	2	2½	3

* Use a variety of fabrics.

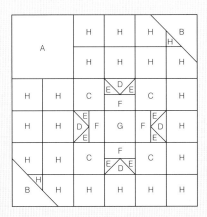

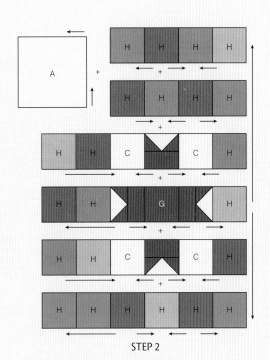

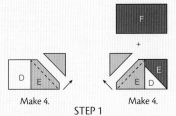

Make 4.   Make 4.

STEP 1   STEP 2   STEP 3

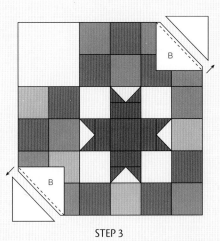

VARIABLE STAR

This block is so versatile that I've included five rotary cut sizes.

USED FOR	SHAPE/ COLOR	NUMBER TO CUT	BLOCK SIZE				
			4"	6"	8"	10"	12"
A	▢	4 ▢	1½	2	2½	3	3½
B	△	4 ▭	1½ x 2½	2 x 3½	2½ x 4½	3 x 5½	3½ x6½
C	◣	8 ◼	1½	2	2½	3	3½
D	▢	1 ▢	2½	3½	4½	5½	6½

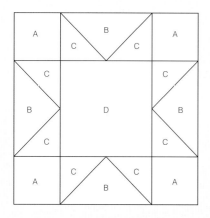

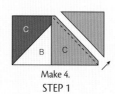

Make 4.
STEP 1

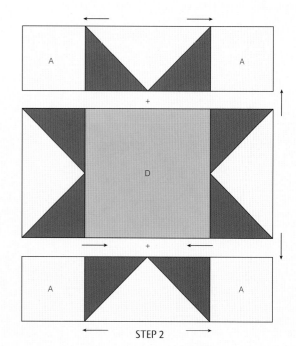

STEP 2

CHRISTMAS WREATH

(Design by Erena Rieflin)

You could replace the center square (A and D) on the 12" block with any 6" block.

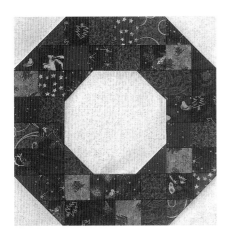
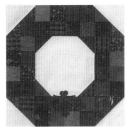
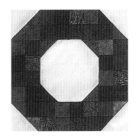

USED FOR	SHAPE/ COLOR	NUMBER TO CUT	BLOCK SIZE			
			6"	8"	10"	12"
A	☐	1 ☐	3½	4½	5½	6½
B	◿	4 ☐	2	2½	3	3½
C	▨ ◣	48* ▤	1¼	1½	1¾	2
D	◣	4* ▨	1½	1¾	2	2¼

* Use a variety of colors.

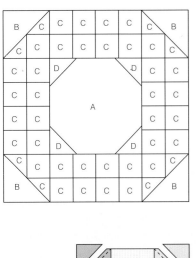

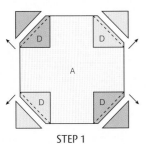

STEP 1

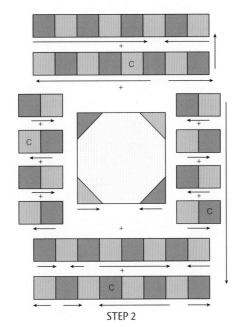

STEP 2

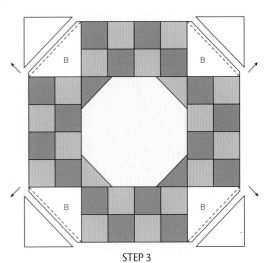

STEP 3

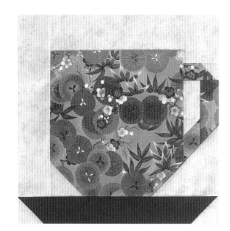

TEACUP

(Design by Karen F. Srebro)

This block will complement the Teapot block (page 48).

USED FOR	SHAPE/ COLOR	NUMBER TO CUT	BLOCK SIZE			
			6"	8"	10"	12"
A		1	1½ X 5¾	2 X 7½	2¼ X 9¼	2½ X 11
B		1	1½ X 4½	2 X 5½	2¼ X 7	2½ X 8½
C		1	1½ X 1⅞	2 X 2⅜	2¼ X 2¾	2½ X 3¼
D		1	1½	1¾	2¼	2½
E		2	1¼	1½	1¾	2
F		1	1	1¼	1⅜	1½
G		1	2½	3¼	4	4½
H		1	1 X 2⅛	1¼ X 2⅝	1⅜ X 3¼	1½ X 3¾
I		1	1 X 1½	1¼ X 2	1⅜ X 2¼	1½ X 2½
J		1	1 X 2¾	1¼ X 3½	1⅜ X 4¼	1½ X 5
K		1	1 X 3⅞	1¼ X 4⅞	1⅜ X 6⅛	1½ X 7¼
L		1	4½ X 4¾	5½ X 6	7 X 7½	8½ X 9
M		1	1¼ X 6½	1½ X 8½	1¾ X 10½	2 X 12½

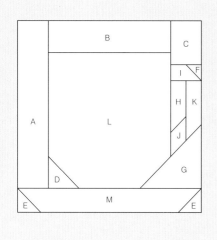 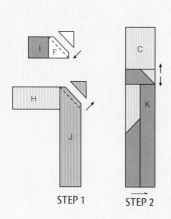 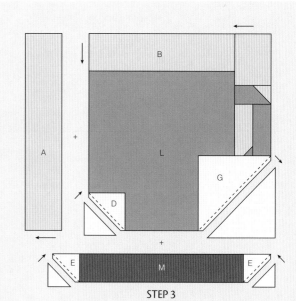

STEP 1

STEP 2

STEP 3

TEA CUP

TIN SOLDIERS
(Design by Erena Rieflin)

Mix and match colors and sizes for a unique wallhanging for
Christmas or to use in a boy's room. Embellish with gold buttons.

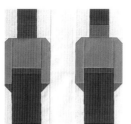

USED FOR	SHAPE/ COLOR	NUMBER TO CUT	BLOCK SIZE			
			6"	9"	12"	15"
A		1	1½ x 6½	2 x 9½	3 x 12½	4 x 15½
B		4	1 x 2⅞	1⅛ x 4⅛	1⅜ x 5¼	1½ x 6½
C		4	1¼ x 1⅞	1⅝ x 2½	1⅞ x 3¼	2⅛ x 4
D		4	¾	⅞	1	1⅛
E		2	1 x 1½	1⅛ x 2	1½ x 2½	1¾ x 3
F		4	1 x 2¾	1⅛ x 3⅞	1⅜ x 5	1½ x 6
G		4	1¼ x 3	1¾ x 4	2 x 5½	2⅜ x 6⅝
H		2	¾ x 2	⅞ x 3	1 x 3½	1⅛ x 4¼
I		2	2	3	3½	4¼
J		2	¾ x 1½	⅞ x 2	1 x 2½	1⅛ x 3
K		4	⅞ x 1¼	1⅛ x 1¾	1¼ x 2	1½ x 2⅜
L		4	1	1⅛	1⅜	1½
M		2	1⅛ x 1½	1½ x 2	1¾ x 2½	2⅛ x 3

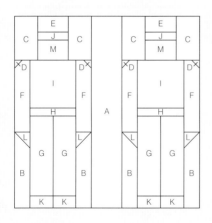

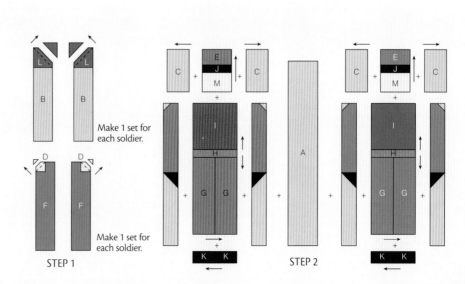

TEAPOT

(Design by Ruth A. Lindhagen)

Use the teapot to make a friendship wallhanging. Have friends choose a color for their teapot and embellish each with their initials.

USED FOR	SHAPE/ COLOR	NUMBER TO CUT	BLOCK SIZE			
			6"	9"	12"	15"
A		2	2 x 3⅞	2¾ x 5½	3½ x 7¼	4¼ x 9
B		2	1¼	1¾	2	2½
C		1	1¼ x 2	1¾ x 2¾	2 x 3½	2½ x 4¼
D		2	1½	2	2½	3
E		1	1½ x 3	2 x 4⅛	2½ x 5½	3 x 6⅝
F		1	2 x 2¼	2¾ x 3⅛	3½ x 4	4¼ x 4⅞
G		2	1¾	2⅜	3	3⅝
H		2	1 x 1¾	1¼ x 2⅜	1½ x 3	1¾ x 3⅝
I		1	1 x 2	1¼ x 2¾	1½ x 3½	1¾ x 4¼
J		1	1 x 3½	1¼ x 5	1½ x 6½	1¾ x 8
K		1	3½ x 5½	5 x 8	6½ x 10½	8 x 13
L		1	2 x 2¾	2¾ x 4	3½ x 5	4¼ x 6
M		2	1 x 2	1¼ x 2¾	1½ x 3½	1¾ x 4¼
N		1	1 x 3	1¼ x 4⅛	1½ x 5½	1¾ x 6⅝
O		2	1¼	1⅝	2	2⅜

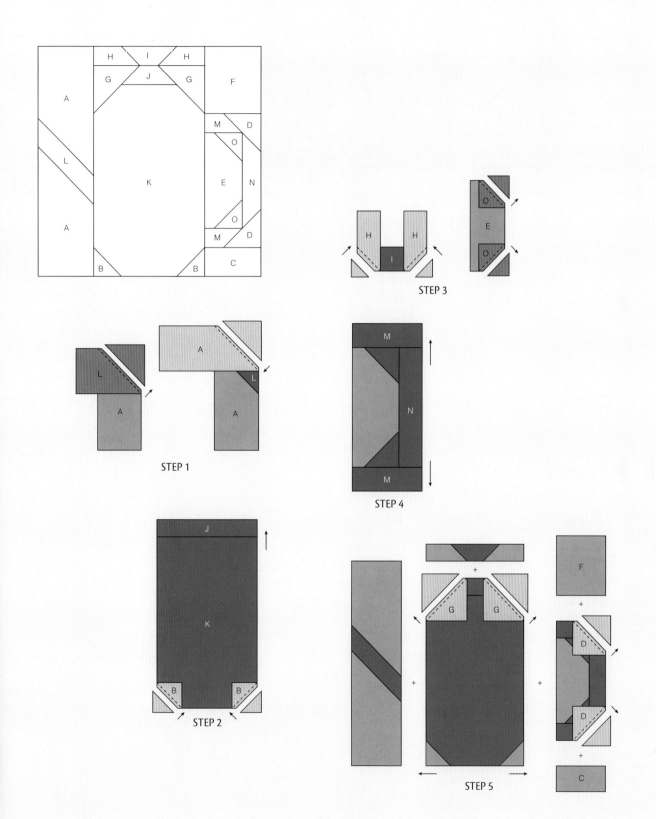

STEP 3

STEP 1

STEP 4

STEP 2

STEP 5

QUILT SHOPPE

(Design by Nancy Johnson-Srebro)

No town would be complete without a quilt shop!

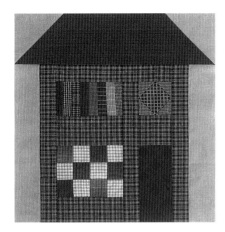

USED FOR	SHAPE/ COLOR	NUMBER TO CUT	BLOCK SIZE			
			6"	**9"**	**12"**	**15"**
A		2	1⅛ x 5	1½ x 7¼	2 x 9½	2⅜ x 11¾
B		2	2	2¾	3½	4¼
C		1	2 x 6½	2¾ x 9½	3½ x 12½	4¼ x 15½
D		2	1 x 5	1¼ x 7¼	1½ x 9½	1¾ x 11¾
E		1	1 x 4¼	1¼ x 6	1½ x 7½	1¾ x 9¼
F		1	1 x 4½	1¼ x 6½	1½ x 8½	1¾ x 10½
G		1	1¼ x 2½	1¾ x 3½	2¼ x 4½	2¾ x 5½
H		1	1¼ x 1¾	1¾ x 2¼	2¼ x 2½	2¾ x 3
I		1	1 x 2½	1¼ x 3½	1¾ x 4½	2 x 5½
J		1	1¾ x 2½	2¼ x 3½	2½ x 4¾	3 x 5¾
K		6 *	1	1¼	1½	1¾
L		1 **	¾ x 1¾	⅞ x 2¼	1 x 2½	1⅛ x 3
M		1	1¾	2¼	2½	3
N		4	1⅛	1⅜	1½	1¾

* Repeat using another color.   ** Repeat using eight different colors.

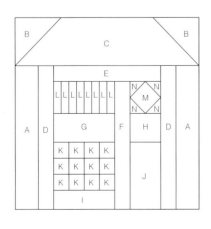

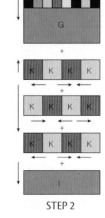

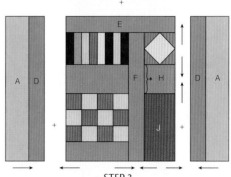

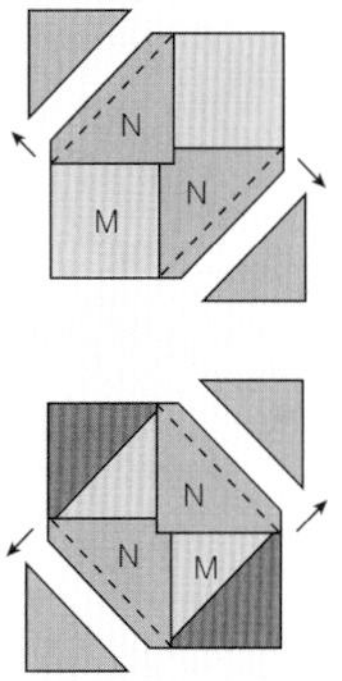

STEP 1   STEP 2   STEP 3
short side of rectangle (H)

FUZZY THE BEAR

(Design by Nancy Johnson-Srebro)

To make a girl bear, embellish with a head band and a bow. To make a boy bear, embellish with a bow tie and a pocket on his coveralls.

USED FOR	SHAPE/ COLOR	NUMBER TO CUT	BLOCK SIZE			
			6"	8"	10"	12"
A		2	1½ x 2½	1⅞ x 3	2¼ x 3¾	2½ x 4½
B		1	1¼ x 3½	1½ x 4½	1¾ x 5¼	2 x 6½
C		1	3¼ x 4¼	4¼ x 5½	5 x 6½	6 x 8
D		2	1¾	2¼	2¾	3
E		1	1¼ x 2½	1½ x 3	1⅞ x 3½	2 x 4½
F		2	1½	1⅞	2¼	2½
G		2	1⅝ x 3¼	2 x 4¼	2½ x 5	2¾ x 6
H		2	1¼ x 1¾	1½ x 2¼	1¾ x 2¾	2 x 3
I		4	1	1¼	1⅜	1½
J		4	⅞	1	1¼	1¼
K		1	1 x 2½	1¼ x 3	1⅜ x 3½	1½ x 4½
L		1	1¾ x 4½	2 x 5¾	2½ x 7	3 x 8½
M		2	1 x 1¼	1⅛ x 1½	1⅜ x 1¾	1½ x 2
Eyes and Nose	● ▼	2*, 1*	See page 11			

*Fuse on after sewing the complete block.

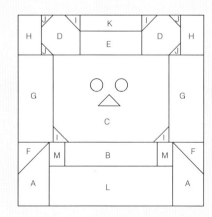

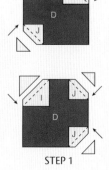

STEP 1

STEP 2

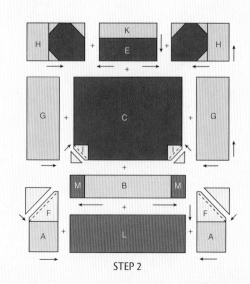

YUMMY APPLE

(Design by Nancy Johnson-Srebro)

Who could resist taking a bite out of this colorful apple?
Mix and match sizes for a bountiful harvest.

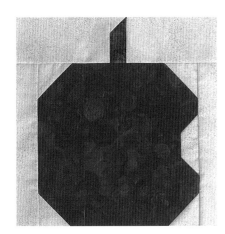

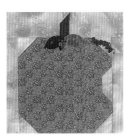

USED FOR	SHAPE/ COLOR	NUMBER TO CUT	BLOCK SIZE			
			6"	8"	10"	12"
A	▭	2 ▭	1⅛ X 5¼	1¼ X 7	1½ X 8½	1¾ X 10
B	◹	4 ▫	1½	1¾	2	2½
C	▽	1 ▭	1 X 2¼	1¼ X 2½	1⅜ X 3½	1½ X 4
D	◹	1 ▫	1	1¼	1½	1½
E	▭	2 ▭	1¾ X 3¼	2 X 4⅛	2½ X 5	3 X 6
F	◣	1 ▪	1 X 1¾	1¼ X 2	1½ X 2½	1½ X 3
G	▽	1 ▬	1 X 5¼	1¼ X 7	1⅜ X 8½	1½ X 10
H	▭	2 ▬	1⅜ X 5¼	1½ X 7	2 X 8½	2¼ X 10
I	▭	2 ▬	1½ X 5¼	2 X 7	2⅛ X 8½	2½ X 10
J	◢◣	2 ▬	1 X 2	1¼ X 2¾	1⅜ X 3	1½ X 3½
K	◣	2 ▪	1	1¼	1⅜	1½

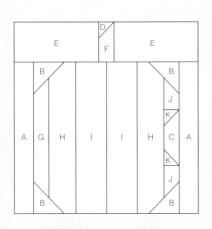

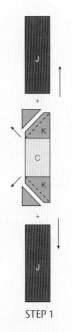

STEP 1

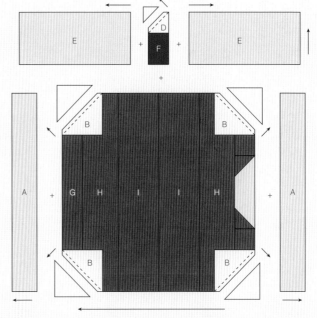

STEP 2

TALL PINES

(Design by Nancy Johnson-Srebro)

You can see this pine tree swaying in the wind. For a scrappy look, use different greens or embellish with Christmas decorations.

USED FOR	SHAPE/ COLOR	NUMBER TO CUT	BLOCK SIZE			
			6"	8"	10"	12"
A		2	2½ x 3⅛	3 x 4	4 x 4⅞	4½ x 5¾
B		2	1½ x 2¼	1⅞ x 2⅞	2⅛ x 3⅜	2½ x 4
C		2	1½ x 2⅝	1⅞ x 3⅜	2⅛ x 4	2½ x 4¾
D		2	1½ x 3	1⅞ x 3⅞	2⅛ x 4⅝	2½ x 5½
E		2	1½ x 3½	1⅞ x 4½	2⅛ x 5½	2½ x 6½
F	▲	1	1½ x 2½	1⅞ x 3¼	2⅛ x 3¾	2½ x 4½
G	▲	1	1½ x 3½	1⅞ x 4½	2⅛ x 5½	2½ x 6½
H	▲	1	1½ x 4¼	1⅞ x 5½	2⅛ x 6¾	2½ x 8
I	▲	1	1½ x 5	1⅞ x 6½	2⅛ x 8	2½ x 9½
J	■	1	1¼ x 2½	1½ x 3	1¾ x 4	2 x 4½

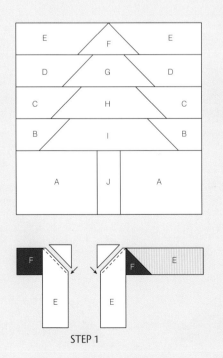

STEP 1

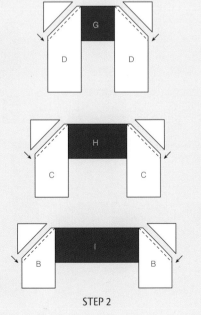

STEP 2

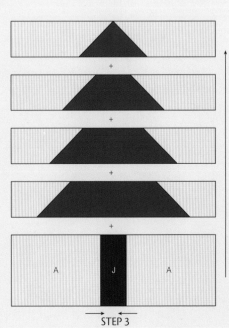

STEP 3

SANTA CLAUS

(Design by Cindy Mundy Cochran)

Young and old have a soft spot for this jolly fella.
Piece him in traditional Christmas colors or create your own St. Nick.

USED FOR	SHAPE/ COLOR	NUMBER TO CUT	BLOCK SIZE 6"	8"	10"	12"
A		2	2 x 2¾	2½ x 3½	3 x 4¼	3½ x 5
B		2	1 x 1¼	1⅛ x 1½	1⅜ x 1¾	1½ x 2
C		2	1¼ x 2¾	1½ x 3½	1¾ x 4¼	2 x 5
D		2	1¼	1½	1¾	2
E		2	2 x 2¾	2½ x 3½	3 x 4¼	3½ x 5
F		1	2 x 5	2½ x 6½	3 x 8	3½ x 9½
G		2	1¼	1½	1¾	2
H		2	1¼ x 2¾	1½ x 3½	1¾ x 4¼	2 x 5
I		1	2¾ x 3½	3½ x 4½	4¼ x 5½	5 x 6½
J		1	1¼ x 5½	1½ x 7¼	1¾ x 8¾	2 x 10½
K		1	2 x 5	2½ x 6½	3 x 8	3½ x 9½
Eyes, mouth and mustache	● ▲ 〰	2*, 1*, 2*	See page 11			

*Fuse on after sewing the complete block..

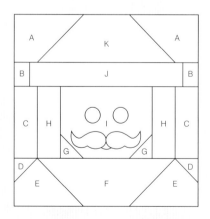

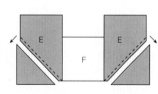
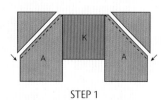

STEP 1

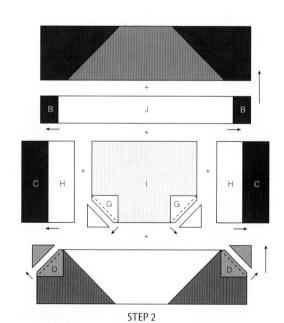

STEP 2

EASTER BASKET

(Design by Nancy Johnson-Srebro)

Fill this Easter basket with colored eggs, bunnies, and lots of jelly beans.

  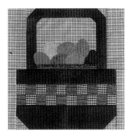

USED FOR	SHAPE/ COLOR	NUMBER TO CUT	BLOCK SIZE			
			6"	9"	12"	15"
A	▭	2	1 x 3½	1¼ x 5	1½ x 6½	1¾ x 8
B	◺	2	1¼	1½	2	2½
C	▭	2	1½ x 3½	2 x 5	2½ x 6½	3 x 8
D	◹	2	1	1¼	1½	1¾
E	▱	1	3 x 3½	4¼ x 5	5½ x 6½	6¾ x 8
F	◣	2	¾	⅞	1	1¼
G	▭	2	1 x 3	1¼ x 4¼	1½ x 5½	1¾ x 6¾
H	◮	1	1 x 4½	1¼ x 6½	1½ x 8½	1¾ x 10½
I	▭	1	1¼ x 5½	1½ x 8	2 x 10½	2¼ x 13
J	⬡	1	1¾ x 5½	2½ x 8	3 x 10½	3¾ x 13
K	▦	10	1	1¼	1½	1¾
L	▢	10	1	1¼	1½	1¾

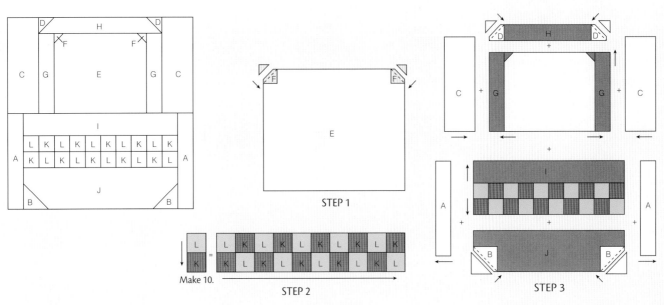

STEP 1

STEP 2

Make 10.

STEP 3

RAINBOW FISH
(Design by Cindy Mundy Cochran)

Use colors you have never thought to use before.
Tropical fish come in many different colors and sizes.

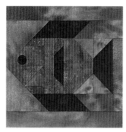  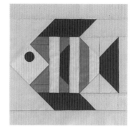

USED FOR	SHAPE/ COLOR	NUMBER TO CUT	BLOCK SIZE			
			6"	8"	10"	12"
A		2	1¼ x 6½	1½ x 8½	1¾ x 10½	2 x 12½
B		2	2¾	3½	4¼	5
C		4	1½	1¾	2	2½
D		2	1½ x 3⅛	1¾ x 3⅞	1¾ x 4½	2¼ x 5½
E		1	1⅛ x 3	1⅜ x 4	1½ x 5½	1½ x 6
F		1	2¼	3	4	4½
G		3	1 x 3	1⅛ x 4	1¼ x 5½	1½ x 6
H		2	1⅜	1¾	2¼	2½
I		2	⅞ x 2¼	1 x 3	1¼ x 4	1¼ x 4½
J		1	1 x 3	1⅛ x 4	1¼ x 5½	1½ x 6
K		2	1⅛ x 1⅜	1⅜ x 1¾	1½ x 2¼	1½ x 2¼
L		1	1⅛ x 2½	1⅜ x 3¼	1½ x 4	1½ x 4½
M		2	1½ x 4⅞	1¾ x 6⅜	1¾ x 7¾	2¼ x 9¼
N		1	1½ x 3	1¾ x 4	2 x 5½	2½ x 6
Eye		1*	See page 11			

*Fuse on after sewing the complete block.

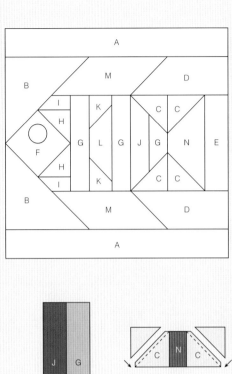

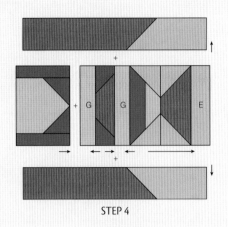

STEP 4

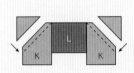

STEP 1

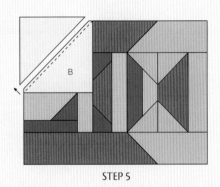

STEP 5

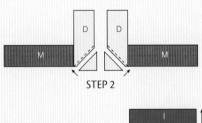

STEP 2

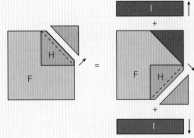

STEP 3

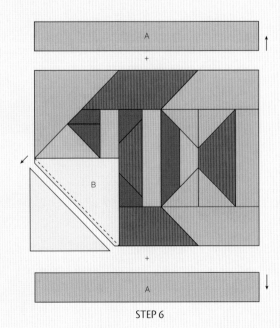

STEP 6

BOO THE GHOST
(Design by Karen F. Srebro)

Kids love ghosts. Make him scary or friendly by changing the color of his eyes and adding a mouth.

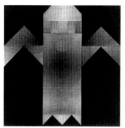  

USED FOR	SHAPE/ COLOR	NUMBER TO CUT	BLOCK SIZE			
			6"	9"	12"	15'
A	▬	2 ▬	1½ x 2½	2 x 3½	2½ x 4½	3 x 5½
B	◣	4 ■	1½	2	2½	3
C	▶	2 ▬	2½ x 4½	3½ x 6½	4½ x 8½	5½ x 10½
D	▲	2 ▬	1 x 1½	1¼ x 2	1½ x 2½	1¾ x 3
E	◣	2 ■	⅞	1⅛	1¼	1½
F	⬠	1 ▭	1¼ x 2½	1¾ x 3½	2 x 4½	2½ x 5½
G	▭	2 ▭	⅞ x 1⅛	1 x 1½	1¼ x 1¾	1⅜ x 2
H	▭	1 ▭	1 x 1⅛	1¼ x 1½	1½ x 1¾	1¾ x 2
I	▭	1 ▭	2½ x 4⅝	3½ x 6½	4½ x 8¾	5½ x 10¾
J	△	2 ▭	1½ x 2½	2 x 3½	2½ x 4½	3 x 5½
K	◺	4 ▢	1½	2	2½	3
L	◺	4 ▢	1	1¼	1½	1¾
M	▬	2 ▬	⅞ x 1⅛	1⅛ x 1½	1¼ x 1¾	1½ x 2

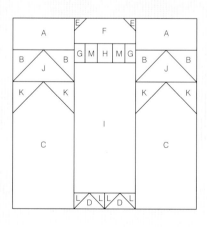

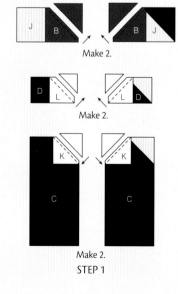

Make 2.
STEP 1

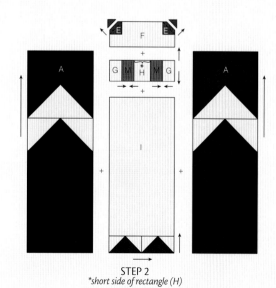

STEP 2
*short side of rectangle (H)

BUTTERFLY
(Design by Frank Srebro)

Spring is here! The color possibilities are endless. Embellish with antennae, too.

USED FOR	SHAPE/ COLOR	NUMBER TO CUT	BLOCK SIZE			
			6"	8"	10"	12"
A	▭	2 ▭	1⅛ X 6½	1½ X 8½	1⅞ X 10½	1¾ X 12½
B	◺	4 □	2½	3	3½	4½
C	⬠	1 ▭	1¼ X 2	1½ X 2½	1¾ X 3	2 X 4
D	◹	2 □	⅞	1	1⅛	1¼
E	▭	1 ▭	1 X 1¼	1¼ X 1½	1½ X 1¾	1½ X 2
F	◣	2 ■	⅞	1	1⅛	1¼
G	⬟	1 ■	1¼ X 4½	1½ X 5¾	1¾ X 7	2 X 8
H		16 ▭	1 X 2	1⅛ X 2½	1¼ X 3	1½ X 3½
I		16 ▭	1 X 2	1⅛ X 2½	1¼ X 3	1½ X 3½

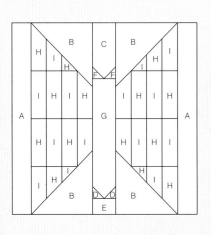

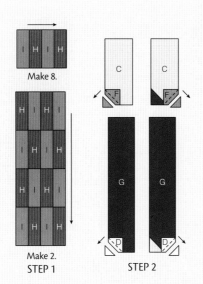

Make 8.

Make 2.
STEP 1

STEP 2

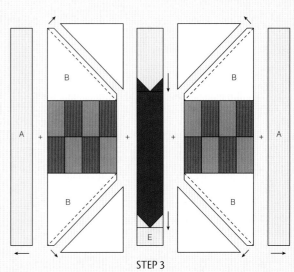

STEP 3

HEART OF AMERICA

(Design by Nancy Johnson-Srebro)

This heart can be done in colors to celebrate any holiday or give to someone special.

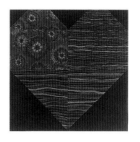

USED FOR	SHAPE/ COLOR	NUMBER TO CUT	BLOCK SIZE			
			6"	8"	10"	12"
A		2	3½	4½	5½	6½
B		1	2½ x 3½	3 x 4½	3¾ x 5½	4½ x 6½
C		1	1½ x 3½	2 x 4½	2¼ x 5½	2½ x 6½
D		1	1½ x 3½	2 x 4½	2¼ x 5½	2½ x 6½
E		1	2½ x 3½	3 x 4½	3¾ x 5½	4½ x 6½
F		4	1½	2	2¼	2½
G		2	3½	4½	5½	6½

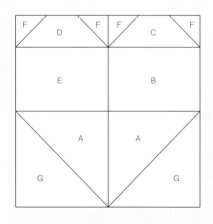

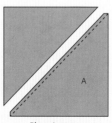

Place A on top of G and stitch. Press toward A. Make 2.

STEP 1

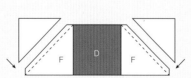

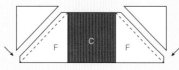

STEP 2

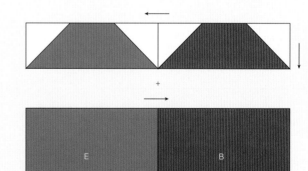

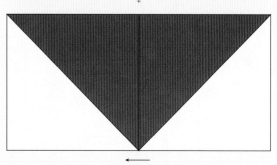

STEP 3

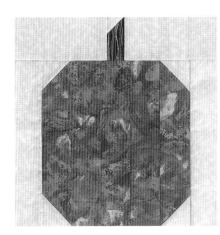

PUMPKIN PATCH

(Design by Nancy Johnson-Srebro)

Create a great fall wallhanging by mixing and matching the different size pumpkins.

USED FOR	SHAPE/ COLOR	NUMBER TO CUT	BLOCK SIZE			
			6"	8"	10"	12"
A		2	1¾ x 3¼	2 x 4⅛	2½ x 5	3 x 6
B		1	1	1¼	1½	1½
C		2	1 x 5¼	1⅜ x 7	1¾ x 8½	2⅛ x 10
D		4	1½	1¾	2	2¼
E		2	1½ x 5¼	1¾ x 7	2 x 8½	2¼ x 10
F		3	1½ x 5¼	1¾ x 7	2 x 8½	2¼ x 10
G		1	1 x 1¾	1¼ x 2	1½ x 2½	1½ x 3

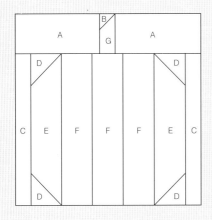

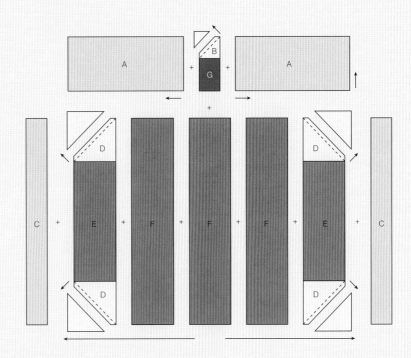

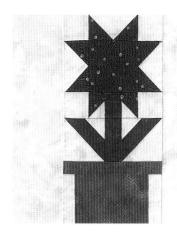

POT OF STARS

(Design by Nancy Johnson-Srebro)

Make this flower shine like a star or be as simple as a summer daisy.

USED FOR	SHAPE/ COLOR	NUMBER TO CUT	BLOCK SIZE			
			6"	8"	10"	12"
A		2	2 x 6½	2½ x 8½	3 x 10½	3½ x 12½
B		2	⅞ x 1⅞	1 x 2⅜	1⅛ x 2¾	1¼ x 3¼
C		2	1¾	2⅛	2⅝	3
D		2	1⅛	1¼	1¾	1¾
E		2	1 x 1¼	1⅛ x 1½	1⅜ x 1¾	1½ x 2
F		4	1¼	1½	1¾	2
G		3	1¼ x 2	1½ x 2½	1¾ x 3	2 x 3½
H		8	1¼	1½	1¾	2
I		1	2	2½	3	3½
J		1	1 x 1¾	1¼ x 2⅛	1¼ x 2⅝	1½ x 3
K		2	1¾	2⅛	2⅝	3
L		1	1 x 1¼	1¼ x 1½	1¼ x 1¾	1½ x 2
M		1	⅞ x 3½	1 x 4½	1⅛ x 5½	1¼ x 6½
N		1	1⅞ x 2¾	2⅜ x 3½	2¾ x 4¼	3¼ x 5

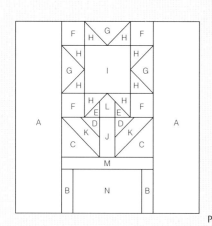

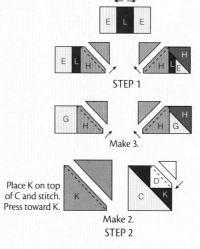

STEP 1

Make 3.

Place K on top of C and stitch. Press toward K.

Make 2.
STEP 2

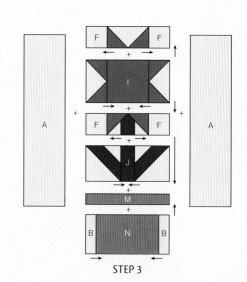

STEP 3

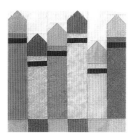

CASEY'S CRAYONS
(Design by Nancy Johnson-Srebro)

This block was designed for our granddaughter, Casey.
She loves to color when she comes to our house.

USED FOR	SHAPE/ COLOR	NUMBER TO CUT	BLOCK SIZE			
			6"	**9"**	**12"**	**15"**
A	◣	12 ■	1	1¼	1½	1¾
B	■	1 ■	1½ x 1⅝	2 x 2⅛	2½ x 2¾	3 x 3⅜
C	■	1 ■	1⅛ x 1½	1½ x 2	1¾ x 2½	2 x 3
D	■	1 ■	1½ x 2	2 x 2¾	2½ x 3½	3 x 4¼
E	■	1 ■	¾ x 1½	⅞ x 2	1 x 2½	1⅛ x 3
F	⬠	1* ▬	1½ x 1⅝	2 x 2⅛	2½ x 2¾	3 x 3⅜
G	▬	1* ▬	1⅛ x 1½	1½ x 2	1¾ x 2½	2 x 3
H	▬	6 ▬	¾ x 1½	⅞ x 2	1 x 2½	1⅛ x 3
I	▬	1* ▬	¾ x 1½	⅞ x 2	1 x 2½	1⅛ x 3
J & J1	▬	1** ▬	1½ x 4¼	2 x 6⅛	2½ x 8	3 x 9⅞
K	▬	1 ▬	1½ x 3⅛	2 x 4½	2½ x 5¾	3 x 7
L	▭	1 ▭	1½ x 3⅝	2 x 5⅛	2½ x 6¾	3 x 8⅜
M	▬	1 ▬	1½ x 2¾	2 x 3⅞	2½ x 5	3 x 6⅛
N	▬	1 ▬	1½ x 4	2 x 5¾	2½ x 7½	3 x 9¼

*Repeat using six different colors.   **Using two different colors, cut one J and one J1.

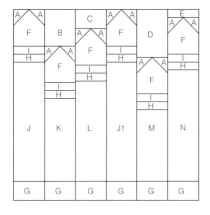

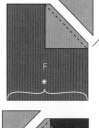

Make 1 of each color.
STEP 1
short side of rectangle (F)

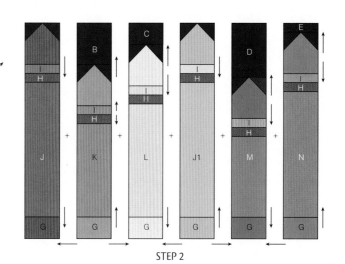

STEP 2

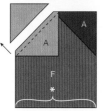

COUNTRY BIRD

(Design by Nancy Johnson-Srebro)

By using different colors, you can easily make a bluebird, a goldfinch, a cardinal, or even a crow. The possibilities are endless.

USED FOR	SHAPE/ COLOR	NUMBER TO CUT	BLOCK SIZE			
			6"	8"	10"	12"
A		1	2½ x 3¾	3¼ x 4¾	4 x 5⅞	4½ x 7
B		2	1⅛ x 1¾	1⅜ x 2⅛	1½ x 2½	1¾ x 3
C		2	1⅞ x 2⅛	2¼ x 2½	2¾ x 3⅛	3¼ x 3¾
D		1	1⅞ x 2⅝	2¼ x 3⅜	2¾ x 3⅝	3¼ x 4¾
E		1	⅞ x 1⅞	1 x 2¼	1⅛ x 2¾	1¼ x 3¼
F		1	1⅞ x 4½	2⅜ x 5¾	2⅞ x 7	3¼ x 8½
G		1	1⅝	1⅞	2⅜	2¾
H		2	1 x 1⅜	1⅛ x 1¾	1⅜ x 2	1½ x 2¼
I		3	1	1⅛	1⅜	1½
J		1	1⅜ x 1½	1¾ x 2	2 x 2¼	2¼ x 2½
K		1	⅞	1	1⅛	1¼
L		1	2⅜ x 2½	3 x 3¼	3⅝ x 4	4¼ x 4½
M		2	1⅛ x 2⅛	1⅜ x 2⅝	1½ x 3¼	1¾ x 3¾
N		1	1⅞ x 4⅞	2¼ x 6⅜	2¾ x 7¾	3¼ x 9¼
O		2	1⅛ x 3½	1⅜ x 4⅝	1½ x 5⅜	1¾ x 6½
P		2	¾ x 1⅞	⅞ x 2¼	1⅛ x 2¾	1 x 3¼
Q		2	1	1¼	1⅜	1½

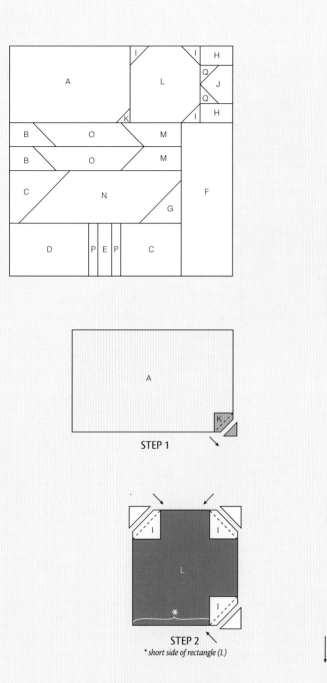

STEP 1

STEP 2
* short side of rectangle (L)

STEP 3
* short side of rectangle (J)

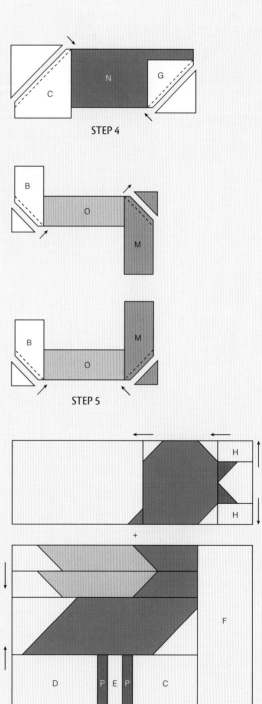

STEP 4

STEP 5

+

STEP 6

SAILBOAT

(Design by Cindy Mundy Cochran)

Think of soft breezes and a clear sunny day while you sail off in this boat.

 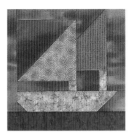 

USED FOR	SHAPE/COLOR	NUMBER TO CUT	BLOCK SIZE			
			6"	9"	12"	15"
A		1	1 x 3½	1¼ x 5	1½ x 6½	1¾ x 8
B		1	1 x 5½	1¼ x 8	1½ x 10½	1¾ x 13
C		1	2	2¾	3½	4¼
D		1	3½	5	6½	8
E		1	1½ x 4½	2 x 6½	2½ x 8½	3 x 10½
F		1	1½ x 1⅝	2 x 2¼	2½ x 2¾	3 x 3¼
G		1	1 x 3⅛	1¼ x 4½	1½ x 5¾	1¾ x 7
H		1	1½ x 2	2 x 2¾	2½ x 3½	3 x 4¼
I		1	1	1¼	1½	1¾
J		1	2 x 3½	2¾ x 5	3½ x 6½	4¼ x 8
K		1	3½	5	6½	8
L		1	⅞ x 1½	1 x 2	1¼ x 2½	1½ x 3
M		1	⅞ x 1	1 x 1¼	1¼ x 1½	1½ x 1¾
N		1	1½ x 5½	2 x 8	2½ x 10½	3 x 13
O		1	1½ x 6½	2 x 9½	2½ x 12½	3 x 15½

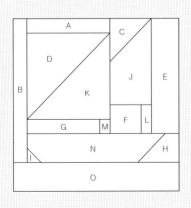

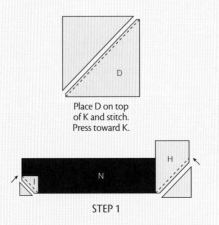

Place D on top of K and stitch. Press toward K.

STEP 1

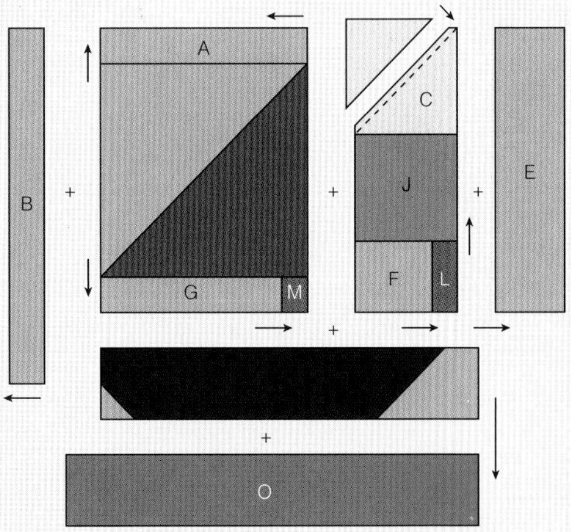

STEP 2

HIP HOP THE BUNNY

(Design by Janet McCarroll)

For added fun, cut a tail from cotton batting to fuse to the block.

USED FOR	SHAPE/ COLOR	NUMBER TO CUT	BLOCK SIZE			
			6"	8"	10"	12"
A		1	1½ x 3½	2 x 4½	2¼ x 5½	2½ x 6½
B		1	2½ x 3	3 x 3⅞	3¾ x 4¾	4½ x 5½
C		3	1¾	2⅛	2⅝	3
D		1	2½	3	3¾	4½
E		2	1	1⅛	1¼	1½
F		1	1⅛	1¼	1½	1¾
G		1	1⅛ x 2⅛	1⅜ x 2⅞	1⅝ x 3⅜	1¾ x 3¾
H		1	2½	3	3¾	4½
I		1	1 x 2½	1⅛ x 3	1¼ x 3¾	1½ x 4½
J		1	1½ x 2½	2 x 3½	2¼ x 4	2½ x 4½
K		1	2½ x 5½	3½ x 7	4 x 8¾	4½ x 10½
L		1	1⅛ x 5½	1⅜ x 7	1⅝ x 8¾	1¾ x 10½
M		1	1⅛ x 6½	1¼ x 8½	1½ x 10½	1¾ x 12½
N		1	1¼ x 6½	1⅜ x 8½	1⅝ x 10½	2 x 12½
Eye		1*	See page 11			

*Fuse on after sewing the complete block.

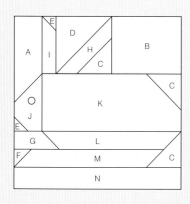 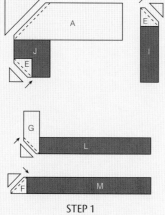 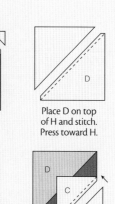 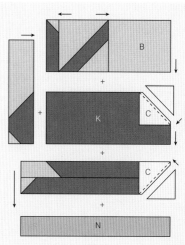

STEP 1

Place D on top of H and stitch. Press toward H.

STEP 2

STEP 3

MR. SCARECROW

(Design by Nancy Johnson-Srebro)

You'll have a blast embellishing this guy! Cut and fuse straw-like hands and feet, and add birds, flowers, and even patches on his overalls.

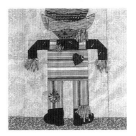

USED FOR	SHAPE/ COLOR	NUMBER TO CUT	BLOCK SIZE			
			6"	9"	12"	15"
A		1	1⅛ x 6½	1½ x 9½	1¾ x 12½	2 x 15½
B		2	1½ x 5⅞	2 x 8½	2½ x 11¼	3 x 14
C		2	1½ x 3¼	2 x 4½	2½ x 6	3 x 7¼
D		1	1 x 2⅜	1¼ x 3¼	1½ x 4¼	1¾ x 5¼
E		2	1 x 1⅛	1¼ x 1½	1½ x 1¾	1¾ x 2¼
F		2	1½ x 2	2¼ x 2¾	2¾ x 3½	3¼ x 4¼
G		4	1	1¼	1½	1¾
H		1	2 x 2½	2¾ x 3	3½ x 4	4¼ x 5
I		3	1 x 1½	1¼ x 2¼	1½ x 2¾	1¾ x 3¼
J		2	1 x 1⅛	1¼ x 1½	1½ x 1¾	1¾ x 2¼
K		1	2 x 2½	2¾ x 3½	3½ x 4½	4¼ x 5½
L		2	1 x 1	⅞ x 1¼	1⅛ x 1½	1⅜ x 1¾
M		2	1¼ x 2⅜	1⅝ x 3¼	2 x 4¼	2⅜ x 5¼
Hat		1	¾ x 2	1 x 2½	1½ x 3½	1¾ x 4½
Brim		1	¼ x 2½	⅜ x 3¼	½ x 4¼	¾ x 5½

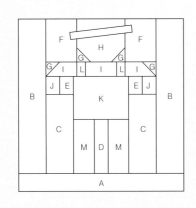

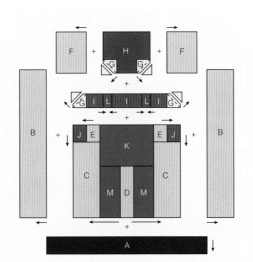

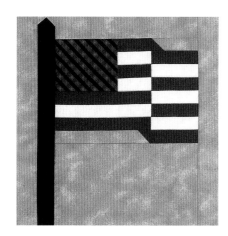

THE FLAG

(Design by Marcia Rickansrud)

Embellish your American flag with a star and watch it blow in the wind.

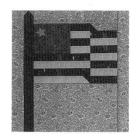

USED FOR	SHAPE/ COLOR	NUMBER TO CUT	BLOCK SIZE			
			6"	8"	10"	12"
A		2	1⅛ x 6½	1¼ x 8½	1½ x 10½	1¾ x 12½
B		1	2⅞ x 4¾	3¾ x 6¼	4½ x 7½	5¼ x 9
C		1	⅞ x 3⅜	1 x 4⅜	1⅛ x 5⅛	1¼ x 6¼
D		1	1⅛ x 4¾	1¼ x 6¼	1½ x 7½	1¾ x 9
E		2	¾	⅞	1	1
F		1	⅞ x 1⅞	1 x 2⅜	1⅛ x 2⅞	1¼ x 3¼
G		1	2 x 2⅜	2½ x 3	3 x 3½	3½ x 4¼
H		2	⅞ x 1½	1 x 1⅞	1⅛ x 2⅛	1¼ x 2½
I		2	⅞	1	1⅛	1¼
J		4	⅞ x 1⅞	1 x 2⅜	1⅛ x 2⅞	1¼ x 3¼
K		2	⅞ x 3⅜	1 x 4⅜	1⅛ x 5⅛	1¼ x 6¼
L		2	⅞ x 1½	1 x 1⅞	1⅛ x 2⅛	1¼ x 2½
M		1	⅞ x 3⅜	1 x 4⅜	1⅛ x 5⅛	1¼ x 6¼
N		3	⅞ x 1⅞	1 x 2⅜	1⅛ x 2⅞	1¼ x 3¼
O		1	1 x 6½	1¼ x 8½	1½ x 10½	1½ x 12½

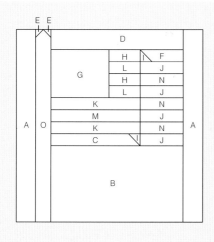

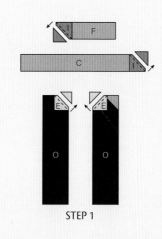

STEP 1

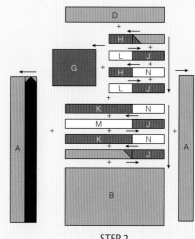

STEP 2

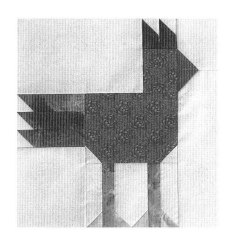

STAR OF THE BARNYARD

(Design by Cindy Mundy Cochran)

This rooster is ready to keep order in any barnyard.

USED FOR	SHAPE/ COLOR	NUMBER TO CUT	BLOCK SIZE			
			6"	8"	10"	12"
A		1	2¾ X 4¼	3⅜ X 5¾	4⅜ X 7	4¾ X 8
B		7	1	1⅛	1¼	1½
C		1	1¾ X 2⅛	2 X 2½	2½ X 3¼	3 X 3½
D		1	1¾ X 4⅞	2 X 6½	2½ X 7¾	3 X 9½
E		2	1 X 2¼	1⅛ X 3⅛	1¼ X 3⅝	1½ X 4¼
F		1	1½ X 2¼	1¾ X 3⅛	2 X 3⅝	2½ X 4¼
G		1	2½ X 2¾	3¼ X 3¾	4 X 4⅜	4½ X 5¼
H		4	1	1⅛	1¼	1½
I		3	1 X 2½	1⅛ X 3¼	1¼ X 4	1½ X 4½
J		2	1⅛	1⅜	1⅝	1¾
K		1	1½ X 1¾	1¾ X 2¼	2 X 2¾	2½ X 3
L		1	2½ X 3¼	3 X 4¼	3½ X 5	4½ X 6
M		2	⅞ X 2¼	1⅛ X 3⅛	1¼ X 3⅝	1¼ X 4¼
N		2	1 X 1½	1⅛ X 1⅝	1¼ X 2⅛	1½ X 2¼

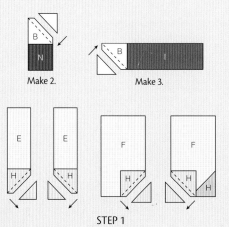 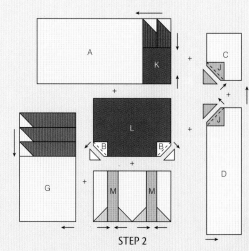

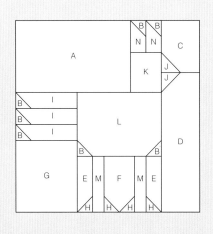

QUILT MAP PROJECTS

While deciding how the blocks could be put together into wallhangings and quilts, I realized that this process resembled a road map. Maps are so important! They give us clear instructions so we can get from point A to point B. The same is true with these Quilt Maps—they will direct you through the assembly process from beginning to end.

These Quilt Maps are a perfect foundation to showcase these blocks. Mix and match them to create your own designs.

Yardage and cutting charts are provided with each Quilt Map. I've overestimated the yardage needed to allow for shrinking of the fabric, squaring up, etc. Also, I allowed 3" for the width of the binding strips even though I usually use 2⅛" strips for a double binding. ALL BORDERS ARE CUT LONGER THAN NEEDED AND SHOULD BE TRIMMED TO FIT. The backing is 4" larger than the size of the wallhanging. These extra allowances will ensure that you do not run short of fabric.

ALL THE CHILDREN OF THE WORLD

30¾" x 42". Made by Nancy Johnson-Srebro. Quilted by Lea Wang.

Quilt Map #1 was used with 10" Max (page 23) and 10" Samantha (page 31) blocks.

I loved making this wallhanging because

my granddaughter, Casey, helped me

choose the fabrics. This simple map

will showcase any 10" block.

QUILT MAP #1

Finished Quilt Size: 30¾" x 42"
Finished Block Size: 10"
Total Blocks Needed: 6

Yardage Chart (Based on 42" fabric)

Yardage for the actual blocks is not included.

Item	Quantity to Buy
Inner Borders & A	½ YARD
*Outer Borders, *Binding & B	1¼ YARDS
Backing	35" X 46"

*Based on cutting lengthwise grain of fabric.

Cutting Chart

Item	Cut Size	# To Cut
A	1¾" x 10½"	7
B	1¾" x 1¾"	2
Inner Side Borders	2" x 23"	2
Inner Top/Bottom Borders	2" x 38"	2
Outer Side Borders	3½" x 26"	2
Outer Top/Bottom Borders	3½" x 43"	2

tip!

This is a quick and easy setting for 10" blocks. If you want to add more blocks, increase the amount of fabric you buy for the lattice strips and borders.

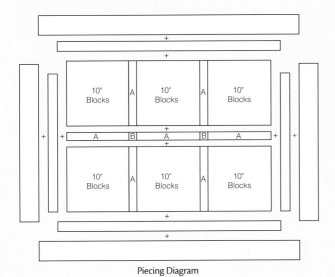

Piecing Diagram

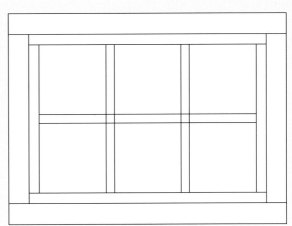

Completed Quilt Diagram

TEA TIME

30¾" x 30¾". Made by Nancy Johnson-Srebro. Quilted by Lea Wang.

Quilt Map #2 was used with 6" Teacup (page 46) and 15" Teapot (page 48) blocks.

It was fun working with oriental-looking

fabrics for the teacups and teapot.

QUILT MAP #2

Finished Quilt Size: 30¾" x 30¾"
Finished Block Sizes: 6" and 15"
Total Blocks Needed: 8

Yardage Chart (Based on 42" fabric)
Yardage for the actual blocks is not included.

Item	Quantity to Buy
*A, *B, *C, *D, *I, *J, *K, *L & *Binding	⅞ YARD
*E, *F, *G, *H	¼ YARD
Backing	35" x 35"

*Based on cutting crosswise grain of fabric.

Cutting Chart

Item	Cut Size	# To Cut
A	2" x 17"	1
B	2" x 18"	1
C	2" x 18"	1
D	2" x 19"	1
E	1½" x 27"	1
F	1" x 27"	1
G	1½" x 27"	1
H	1" x 27"	1
I	3½" x 27"	1
J	2¼" x 27"	1
K	3½" x 32"	1
L	2¼" x 32"	1

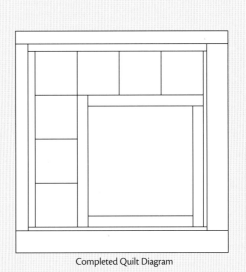

There's nothing ordinary looking about this wallhanging. Different width borders give it a great off-set look.

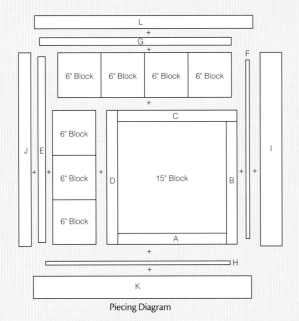

Piecing Diagram

Completed Quilt Diagram

DOLL HOUSE OF BEARS

27" x 31". Made by Nancy Johnson-Srebro. Quilted by Christine Husak.

Quilt Map #3 was used with 6" Fuzzy the Bear (page 51) blocks.

I really like this doll house Quilt Map. Any

of the people or animal blocks in this book

would look great in this setting.

QUILT MAP #3

Finished Quilt Size: 27" x 31"
Finished Block Size: 6"
Total Blocks Needed: 6

Yardage Chart (Based on 42" fabric)
Yardage for the actual blocks is not included.

Item	Quantity to Buy
A & C	¼ YARD
B	2" x 4"
*D & *E	¼ YARD
*F, G, H, I & *Binding	¾ YARD
J	¼ YARD
K	9" x 12"
Backing	31" x 35"

*Based on cutting crosswise grain of fabric.

Cutting Chart

Item	Cut Size	# To Cut
A	1½" x 6½"	7
B	1½" x 1½"	2
C	2" x 20½"	1
D	2¼" x 15"	2
E	3½" x 24"	1
F	4" x 18"	2
G	6" x 8"	2
H	4" x 10¾"	2
I	4" x 4½"	1
J	6" x 27"	1
K	3½" x 4"	2

tip!

Almost any 6" block would look good in this arrangement. You could even turn it into a greenhouse, a chicken coop, or a doghouse.

ROOF SECTION

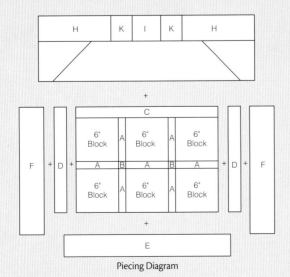

Piecing Diagram

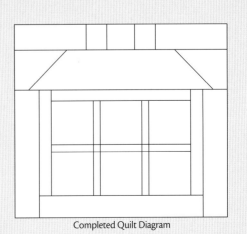

Completed Quilt Diagram

CAT WALK

49½" x 49½". Made by Nancy Johnson-Srebro. Quilted by Christine Husak.

Quilt Map #4 was used with 9" Scaredy-Cat (page 19) blocks.

My daughter Karen faxed me this block design

from her college dorm room early one morning.

When I saw her sketch, I knew it was a winner.

QUILT MAP #4

Finished Quilt Size: 49½" x 49½"
Finished Block Size: 9"
Total Blocks Needed: 8

Yardage Chart (Based on 42" fabric)
Yardage for the actual blocks is not included.

Item	Quantity to Buy
A & B	⅜ YARD
C	1 YARD
*Borders & *Binding	1½ YARDS
Backing	54" X 54"

*Based on cutting lengthwise grain of fabric.

Cutting Chart

Item	Cut Size	# To Cut
A	1¾" x 9½"	8
B	1¾" X 10¾"	8
C	10¾" X 10¾"	8
Side Borders	4½" X 43"	2
Top/Bottom Borders	4½" X 51"	2

The zigzag setting will give movement to any block you use.

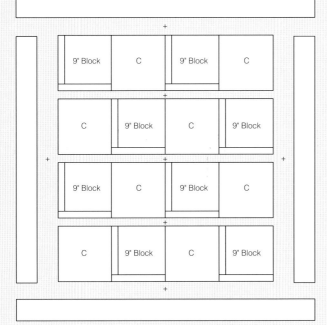

Piecing Diagram

A | 9" Block

+

B

Make 8.

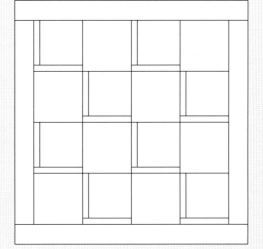

Completed Quilt Diagram

THE QUILT PARTY
27½" x 36½". Made by Nancy Johnson-Srebro. Quilted by Marcia Stevens.

Quilt Map #5 was used with 6" Sewing Machine (page 18),
12" Country Cottage (page 39), and 15" Quilt Shoppe (page 50) blocks.

Every year I invite a few close friends to my

home for a four-day quilting retreat. When

I was working on this wallhanging, I couldn't

help but think of all the fun times we've had.

QUILT MAP #5

Finished Quilt Size: 27½" x 36½"
Finished Block Sizes: 6", 12", and 15"
Total Blocks Needed: 4

Yardage Chart (Based on 42" fabric)

Yardage for the actual blocks is not included.

Item	Quantity to Buy
A	⅛ YARD
B	4" X 4" SQUARE
C	⅛ YARD
*Inner Borders	¼ YARD
*Outer Borders & *Binding	⅞ YARD
Backing	32" X 41"

*Based on cutting crosswise grain of fabric.

Cutting Chart

Item	Cut Size	# To Cut
A	2¼" x 6½"	2
B	2¼" x 3½"	1
C	1¾" x 15½"	1
Inner Side Borders	1¾" x 20"	2
Inner Top/ Bottom Borders	1¾" x 31"	2
Outer Side Borders	3¾" x 22"	2
Outer Top/Bottom Borders	3¾" x 39"	2

This is a quick and easy arrangement—perfect for gift giving!

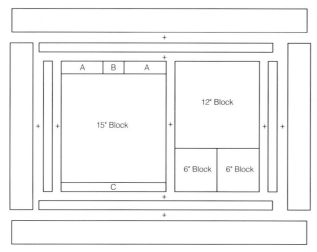

Piecing Diagram

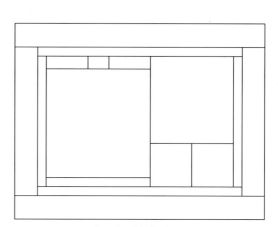

Completed Quilt Diagram

SPRINGTIME IN PENNSYLVANIA

29" x 45¾". Made by Nancy Johnson-Srebro. Quilted by Christine Husak.

Quilt Map #6 was used with 6" Butterfly (page 59), 6" Tulips Galore (page 13),
and 15" Magic Watering Can (page 28) blocks.

QUILT MAP #6

Finished Quilt Size: 29" x 45¾"
Finished Block Sizes: 6" and 15"
Total Blocks Needed: 7

Yardage Chart (Based on 42" fabric)
Yardage for the actual blocks is not included.

Item	Quantity to Buy
*A, *B, C, D & E	½ YARD
F & G	⅛ YARD
H	⅛ YARD
*Borders & *Binding	⅞ YARD
Backing	33" x 50"

*Based on cutting crosswise grain of fabric.

Cutting Chart

Item	Cut Size	# To Cut
A	3½" x 15½"	2
B	3½" x 21½"	2
C	2" x 6½"	3
D	2" x 8"	2
E	2" x 7½"	2
F	1½" x 1½"	2
G	1½" x 18½"	1
H	2¾" x 21½"	1
Side Borders	4¼" x 39"	2
Top/Bottom Borders	4¼" x 30"	2

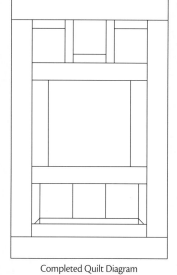

tip!

This is a great wallhanging if you love to embellish. If you want more of a country feeling, use a contrasting fabric for the A and B pieces. You can create many different looks with this Quilt Map.

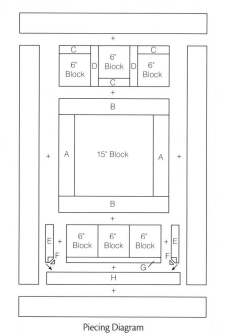

Piecing Diagram

Completed Quilt Diagram

FIRST DAY OF SCHOOL

34" x 40". Made by Nancy Johnson-Srebro. Quilted by Christine Husak.

Quilt Map #7 was used with 6" Yummy Apple (page 52), 6" The Flag (page 69),
6" Tall Pines (page 53), 8" Heart of America (page 60), 8" Max (page 23),
8" Samantha (page 31), 8" Variable Star (page 44), and 12" Schoolhouse (page 16) blocks.

This fun wallhanging brought back memories

of our children starting school. I chose warm

country fabrics with an occasional bright

color thrown in to give some spark.

QUILT MAP #7

Finished Quilt Size: 34" x 40"
Finished Block Sizes: 6", 8", and 12"
Total Blocks Needed: 10

Yardage Chart (Based on 42" fabric)
Yardage for the actual blocks is not included.

Item	Quantity to Buy
A	Various Scraps 2½" SQUARE
B, C & D	⅜ YARD
*Borders & *Binding	1 YARD
Backing	38" X 44"

*Based on cutting crosswise grain of fabric.

Cutting Chart

Item	Cut Size	# To Cut
A	2½" x 2½"	34
B	1½" x 30½"	2
C	2½" x 12½"	1
D	2½" x 16½"	1
Side Borders	4¼" x 34"	2
Top/Bottom Borders	4¼" x 36"	2

tip!

This is a great Quilt Map for using three different-size blocks. Mix and match and create your own personal wallhanging.

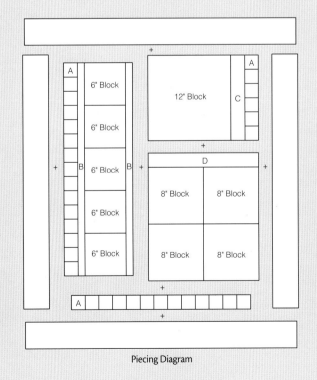

Piecing Diagram

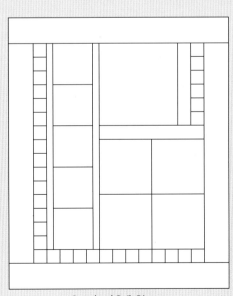

Completed Quilt Diagram

CHRISTMAS MEMORIES
32" x 38". Made and quilted by Janet McCarrroll.

Quilt Map #8 was used with 6" Locomotive (page 24),
6" Variable Star (page 44), 6" Christmas Wreath (page 45),
6" Tin Soldiers (page 47), 6" Toy Horse (page 37),
6" Santa Claus (page 54), 6" Noah's Ark (page 36),
12" Angel of Love (page 20), and 12" Nutcracker (page 35) blocks.

Janet's comments: Memories of past Christmases are very dear to me. I come from a large family and there was always a lot of noise, gifts, and fun at that time of the year.

SPRING IS HERE
32" x 38". Made and quilted by Erena Rieflin.

Quilt Map #8 was used with 6" Tulips Galore (page 13),
6" Country Bird (page 64), 6" Butterfly (page 59),
6" Star of the Barnyard (page 70), 6" Penny the Hen (page 40),
12" Magic Watering Can (page 28), and 12" Birdhouse (page 26) blocks.

In Michigan, the winters are long and cold and I am always looking forward to springtime with all the blooming trees, bushes, and bulbs. I love to appliqué, and enjoyed adding the flowers to the Magic Watering Can block and the vine, berries, and bird to the Bird House block.

QUILT MAP #8

Finished Quilt Size: 32" x 38"
Finished Block Sizes: 6" and 12"
Total Blocks Needed: 10

Yardage Chart (Based on 42" fabric)
Yardage for the actual blocks is not included.

Item	Quantity to Buy
A	⅛ YARD
B	⅛ YARD
C	⅛ YARD
*Borders & *Binding	⅞ YARD
Backing	36" X 42"

*Based on cutting crosswise grain of fabric.

Cutting Chart

Item	Cut Size	# To Cut
A	2½" x 2½"	12
B	2½" x 2½"	12
C	1½" x 24½"	2
Side Borders	4¼" x 32"	2
Top/Bottom Borders	4¼" x 34"	2

tip!

The 12" blocks and checkered section complement the different 6" blocks.

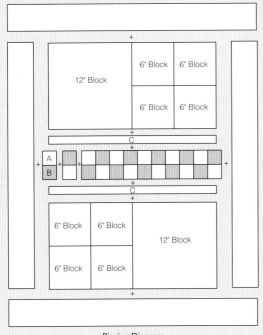

Piecing Diagram

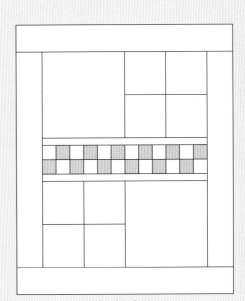

Completed Quilt Diagram

BARNYARD EXPRESS

41" x 53". Made by Nancy Johnson-Srebro. Quilted by Christine Husak and Lea Wang.

Quilt Map #9 was used with 6" Penny the Hen (page 40), 6" Star of the Barnyard (page 70),
6" Patches the Cow (page 34), 8" Tall Pines (page 53), and 15" The Homestead (page 38) blocks.

I spent a lot of childhood time around

my grandmother's farm. I enjoy farm

animals, so it was only natural to use

chicken, cow, and rooster blocks in a

wallhanging. I also love pine trees.

QUILT MAP #9

Finished Quilt Size: 41" x 53"
Finished Block Sizes: 6", 8", and 15"
Total Blocks Needed: 19

Yardage Chart (Based on 42" fabric)
Yardage for the actual blocks is not included.

Item	Quantity to Buy
A & B	⅛ YARD
C, D & E	¼ YARD
F, *G, *H & *Binding	1½ YARDS
Backing	45" X 57"

*Based on cutting crosswise grain of fabric.

Cutting Chart

Item	Cut Size	# To Cut
A	1" x 15½"	2
B	1" x 16½"	2
C	1¾" x 6½"	4
D	2" x 6½"	2
E	1½" x 18½"	4
F	9¾" x 12¾"	4
G	4¾" x 34½"	2
H	4¾" x 16½"	2

This is a wonderful

Quilt Map to highlight

a special 15" block

in the center.

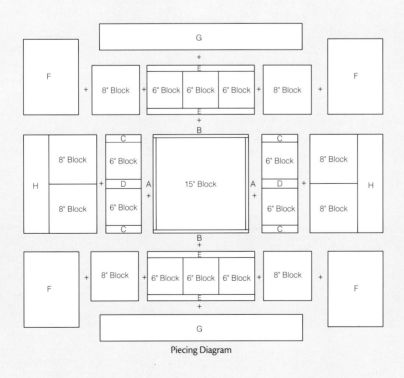

Piecing Diagram

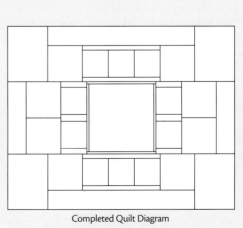

Completed Quilt Diagram

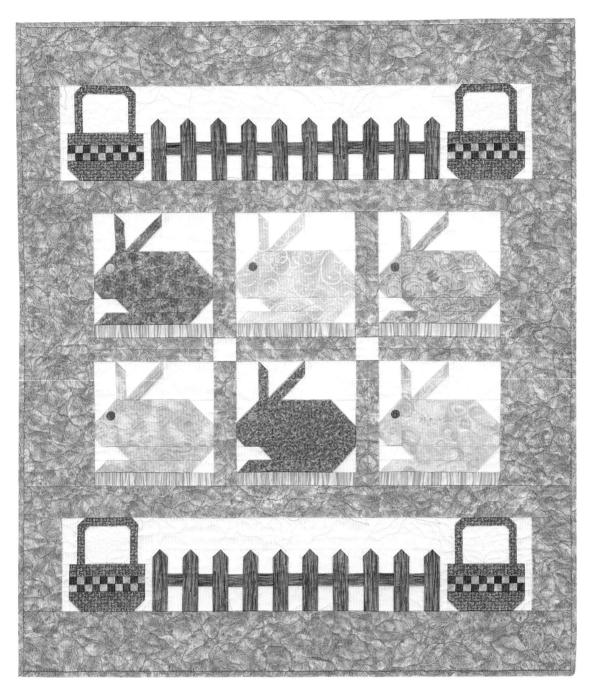

EASTER TIME

37" x 42". Made by Nancy Johnson-Srebro. Quilted by Brenda Leino.

Quilt Map #10 was used with 6" Easter Basket (page 55) and 8" Hip Hop the Bunny (page 67) blocks.

As a child, Easter meant putting on my

black patent-leather shoes and white

gloves, going to church, having Easter

egg hunts, and eating lots of jelly beans.

QUILT MAP #10

Finished Quilt Size: 37" x 42"
Finished Block Sizes: 6" and 8"
Total Blocks Needed: 10

Yardage Chart (Based on 42" fabric)

Yardage for the actual blocks is not included.

Item	Quantity to Buy
*A, B, *C, D, *E & *Binding	1⅜ YARDS
F, G, H & I	⅜ YARD
J & K	¼ YARD
Backing	41" x 46"

*Based on cutting crosswise grain of fabric.

Cutting Chart

Item	Cut Size	# To Cut
A	4½" x 38"	2
B	3¼" x 6½"	4
C	5¼" x 19"	2
D	2" x 8½"	7
E	2½" x 38"	2
F	2½" x 19½"	2
G	1½" x 2⅛"	36
H	1" x 1"	40
I	2" x 2"	2
J	1½" x 4½"	20
K	1¼" x 1½"	18

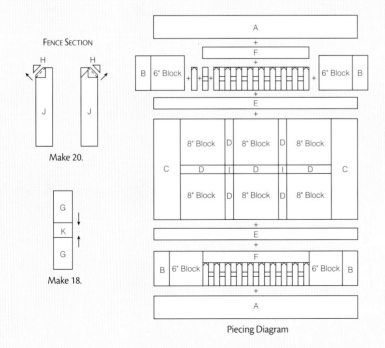

Piecing Diagram

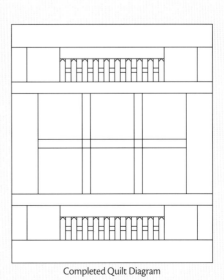

Completed Quilt Diagram

AMISH DELIGHT

27½" x 37½". Made and quilted by Ruth A. Lindhagen.

Quilt Map #11 was used with 6" Pumpkin Patch (page 61), 6" Scaredy-Cat (page 19), 6" Yummy Apple (page 52), two sections of 9" Town Houses (page 42), 9" Mr. Scarecrow, deleting the side strips (B) and trimming the length of A to fit (page 68), 9" School Bus (page 22), and 9" Boo the Ghost (page 58) blocks.

Ruth's comments: I have always associated

trips to the Amish country with the colorful

season of autumn. Fond memories are

brought to mind of crisp autumn days with

falling leaves, flying geese, pumpkins, apples,

school buses, scarecrows, and Halloween.

QUILT MAP #11

Finished Quilt Size: 27½" x 37½"
Finished Block Sizes: 6", 6"x 9", and 9"
Total Blocks Needed: 7

Yardage Chart (Based on 42" fabric)
Yardage for the actual blocks is not included.

Item	Quantity to Buy
A, B, C, D, E, F & *Borders	⅞ YARD
G	¼ YARD
*Binding	⅜ YARD
Backing	32" X 42"

*Based on cutting crosswise grain of fabric.

Cutting Chart

Item	Cut Size	# To Cut
A	1½" x 9½"	1
B	1½" x 19½"	2
C	1½" x 6½"	1
D	1½" x 12½"	1
E	3½" x 3½"	4
F	2" x 2"	32
G	2" x 3½"	16
Side Borders	4½" x 21"	2
Top/Bottom Borders	4½" x 39"	2

The flying geese add

a lot of movement

and excitement

to this setting.

FLYING GEESE SECTION

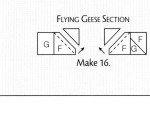

Make 16.

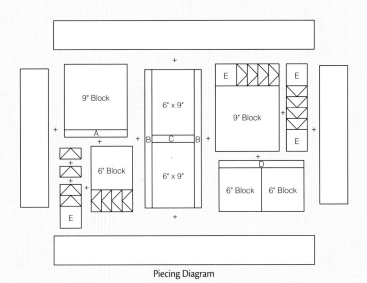

Piecing Diagram

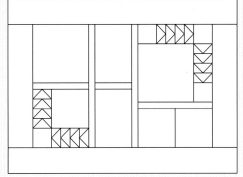

Completed Quilt Diagram

CAMPBELL'S BEACH HOUSE TO THE RESCUE

25" x 32". Made by Nancy Johnson-Srebro. Quilted by Marcia Stevens.

Quilt Map #12 was used with 4" Variable Star (page 44), 6" Pinwheel Flowers, used as two separate flowers (page 21),
6" Rainbow Fish (page 56), 9" Sailboat (page 66), and 12" Campbell's Beach House (page 32) blocks.

Our friends Bonnie and Arlington Campbell have

a wonderful beach house in Virginia. During the

summer they graciously invite my husband and

me there for some rest and relaxation.

QUILT MAP #12

Finished Quilt Size: 25" x 32"
Finished Block Sizes: 4", 3"x 6", 6", 9", and 12"
Total Blocks Needed: 6

Yardage Chart (Based on 42" fabric)
Yardage for the actual blocks is not included.

Item	Quantity to Buy
A, B & *Inner Borders	⅜ YARD
*Outer Borders & *Binding	¾ YARD
Backing	29" x 36"

*Based on cutting crosswise grain of fabric.

Cutting Chart

Item	Cut Size	# To Cut
A	1½" x 9½"	1
B	1½" x 4½"	2
Inner Borders	2½" x 24"	4
Outer Borders	3¼" x 28"	4

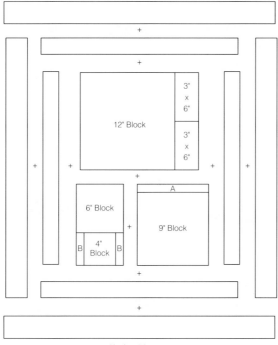

Piecing Diagram

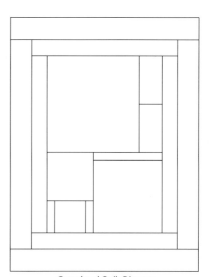

Completed Quilt Diagram

DANCE THE NIGHT AWAY

44" x 44". Made by Nancy Johnson-Srebro. Quilted by Christine Husak.

Quilt Map #13 was used with 9" and 15" Ballerina (page 14) blocks.

I remember the excitement when our daughter had

her first dance recital many years ago. Now our

granddaughter will be starting dance classes!

QUILT MAP #13

Finished Quilt Size: 44" x 44"
Finished Block Sizes: 9" and 15"
Total Blocks Needed: 4

Yardage Chart (Based on 42" fabric)
Yardage for the actual blocks is not included.

Item	Quantity to Buy
*A, *B, *C & *D	⅝ YARD
*E, *F & G	⅝ YARD
H, I, J & K	⅝ YARD
*Inner Border & *Binding	⅝ YARD
Backing	48" x 48"

*Based on cutting crosswise grain of fabric.

Cutting Chart

Item	Cut Size	# To Cut
A	4¼" x 20"	2
B	4¼" x 24"	2
C	2½" x 15½"	2
D	2½" x 17½"	2
E	4¼" x 20"	2
F	4¼" x 24"	2
G	2½" x 2½"	28
H	2½" x 2½"	28
I	5½" x 8½"	4
J	4½" x 4½"	8
K	2½" x 2½"	4
Inner Border	1½" x 38"	4

PINWHEEL BLOCK

 Place H square on top of G square. Sew and press to G. Make 28.

 Make 4.

 Make 12.

Make 4.

Make 4.

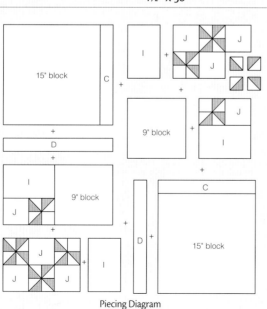

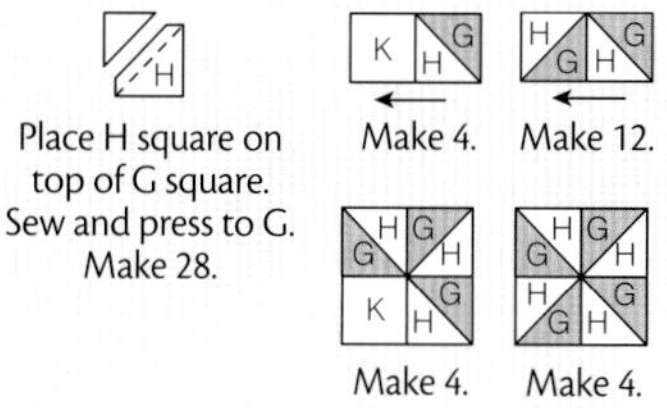

Piecing Diagram

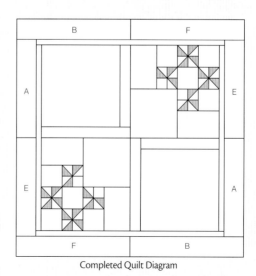

Completed Quilt Diagram

SNOW FAMILY

34½" x 36½". Made by Elsie Mundy and Cindy Mundy Cochran. Quilted by Lea Wang.

Quilt Map #14 was used with 4" Variable Star (page 44), 6", 8", 10", and 12" Snow Family (page 17) blocks.

Cindy's comments: I remember the excitement of setting

out to build the perfect snowman with clothing, trinkets,

and all manner of oddities my mom would gladly let me

borrow. In a child's eyes my friend would last forever.

QUILT MAP #14

Finished Quilt Size: 34½" x 36½"
Finished Block Sizes: 4", 6", 8", 10", and 12"
Total Blocks Needed: 13

Yardage Chart (Based on 42" fabric)

Yardage for the actual blocks is not included.

Item	Quantity to Buy
A, C, D, E & F	¼ YARD
B	2½" x 2½" VARIOUS SCRAPS
*Inner Borders	¼ YARD
*Outer Borders & *Binding	⅞ YARD
Backing	39" X 41"

*Based on cutting crosswise grain of fabric.

Cutting Chart

Item	Cut Size	# To Cut
A	1½" X 1½"	16
B	2½" X 2½"	16
C	1½" X 4½"	8
D	2½" X 4½"	1
E	2½" X 6½"	1
F	2½" X 10½"	1
Inner Borders	1½" X 29"	4
Side Outer Borders	4½" X 28"	2
Top/Bottom Outer Borders	4½" X 39"	2

tip!

This setting showcases many different blocks. The snowball block lends extra excitement to this Quilt Map.

Make 16.　　Make 4.

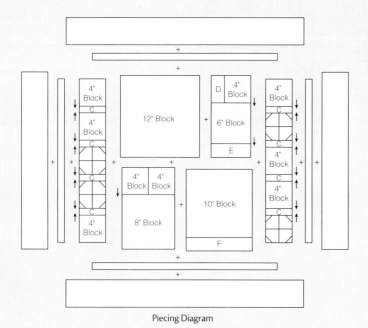

Piecing Diagram

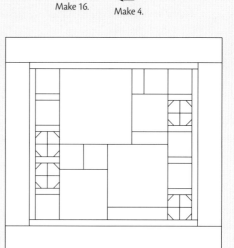

Completed Quilt Diagram

WATCHING EACH OTHER

34½" x 49¼". Made by Janet McCarrroll. Quilted by Lea Wang.

Quilt Map #15 was used with one 6" and two 8" Pinwheel Flowers (6" flower stitched between two 8" flowers page 21), 6" Country Bird (page 64), 6" Cool Cat (page 12), and 8" and 10" Birdhouse (page 26) blocks.

QUILT MAP #15

Finished Quilt Size: 34½" x 49¼"
Finished Block Sizes: 6", 3"x 6", 8", 4"x 8", and 10"
Total Blocks Needed: 12

Yardage Chart (Based on 42" fabric)
Yardage for the actual blocks is not included.

Item	Quantity to Buy
A, B, C, D, E, F & G	½ YARD
*H & *I	¼ YARD
J	⅛ YARD
*Outer Borders & *Binding	1 YARD
Backing	39" X 54"

*Based on cutting crosswise grain of fabric.

Cutting Chart

Item	Cut Size	# To Cut
A	4½" x 6½"	2
B	2½" x 8½"	1
C	2½" x 10½"	1
D	8½" x 12¾"	2
E	2½" x 3½"	2
F	1¾" x 8½"	2
G	1¾" x 1¾"	4
H	1¾" x 24"	2
I	2" x 16½"	1
J	2¾" x 26½"	1
Side Borders	4½" x 42"	2
Top/Bottom Borders	4½" x 36"	2

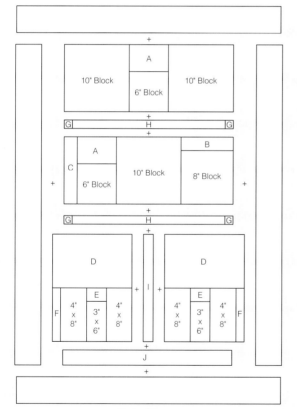

Piecing Diagram

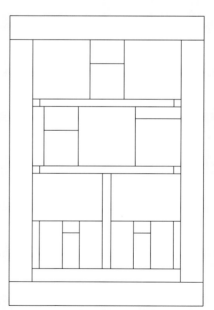

Completed Quilt Diagram

tip!

This Quilt Map allows you to showcase many different-size blocks and add wonderful embellishments too!

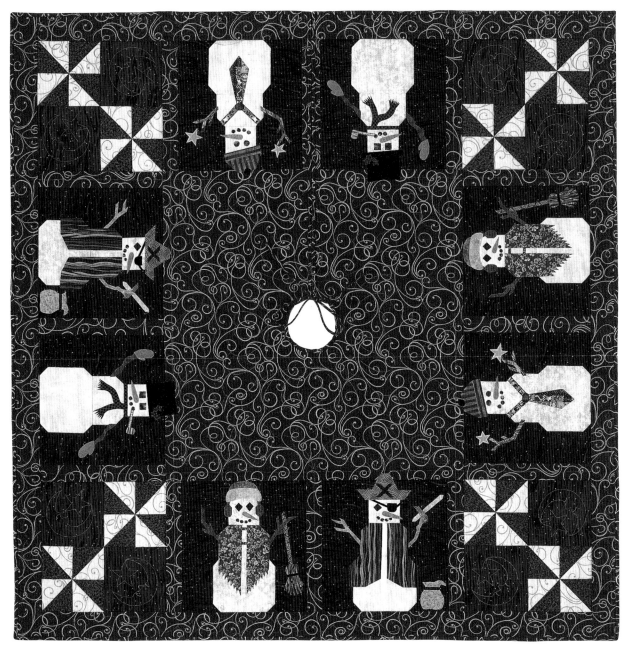

FANTASY CHRISTMAS TREE SKIRT

56½" x 56½". Made by Nancy Johnson-Srebro. Embellishment designs by Cindy Mundy Cochran.
Quilted by Lea Wang. Quilt Map #16 was used with 12" Snow Family (page 17) blocks.

There are four different snow people with

fused embellishments: Papa with his ski cap,

Mama with her shawl; Rudy the Pirate,

and the traditional snowman.

QUILT MAP #16

Finished Quilt Size: 56½" x 56½"
Finished Block Size: 12"
Total Blocks Needed: 8

Yardage Chart (Based on 42" fabric)
Yardage for the actual blocks is not included.

Item	Quantity to Buy
A	⅜ YARD
B	⅜ YARD
C	½ YARD
D, E, *Borders & *Binding	2½ YARDS
Backing	61" x 61"

*Based on cutting borders and outside edge binding lengthwise grain of the fabric.
 Circle binding and ties will need to be cut on the bias. Allow 18" in length for each tie.

Cutting Chart

Item	Cut Size	# To Cut
A	3½" x 3½"	32
B	3½" x 3½"	32
C	6½" x 6½"	8
D	2" x 12½"	12
E	29" x 29"	1
Side Borders	2¼" x 54"	2
Top/Bottom Borders	2¼" x 58"	2

tip!

After quilting, cut a 5" diameter circle in the center of the skirt. Also, rotary cut straight back to the outside edge of the skirt. (See the completed quilt diagram.)

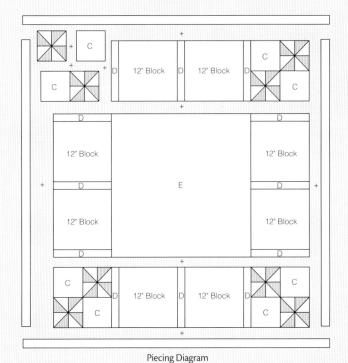

Piecing Diagram

Place B square on top of A square. Sew and press to A. Make 32.

Make 16.

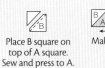
Make 8.

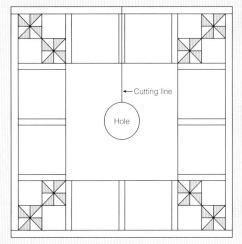

←Cutting line

Hole

Completed Quilt Diagram

KEEPSAKE STAR

72½" x 87½". Made by Nancy Johnson-Srebro. Quilted by Brenda Leino.

Quilt Map #17 was used with 12" Variable Star (page 44) blocks.

I wanted the background to have lots of movement,

so I used fabric from my Keepsake line by Benartex.

Notice that three of the smaller stars are a lighter

color, giving even more movement.

QUILT MAP #17

Finished Quilt Size: 72½" x 87½"
Finished Block Size: 12"
Total Blocks Needed: 20

Yardage Chart (Based on 42" fabric)
Yardage for the actual blocks is not included.

Item	Quantity to Buy
B & C	⅝ YARD
Inner Borders	¾ YARD
A, *Outer Borders & *Binding	3¼ YARDS
Backing	77" x 92"

*Based on cutting lengthwise grain of the fabric.

Cutting Chart

Item	Cut Size	# To Cut
**Inner Side Borders	2½" x 40"	4
**Inner Top/Bottom Borders	2½" x 30"	4
Outer Borders	6" x 78"	4
A	3½" x 12½"	31
B	2" x 2"	96
C	3½" x 3½"	12

**You will have to piece this border.

Choose one block or mix and match a variety of blocks for a sampler look. The stars in the setting will make your quilt shine!

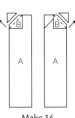

Make 14.

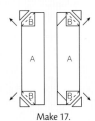

Make 17.

Piecing Diagram

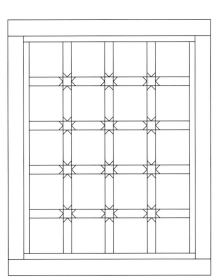

Completed Quilt Diagram

PALACE IN THE PINES
80" x 84". Made by Nancy Johnson-Srebro. Quilted by Lea Wang.

Quilt Map #18 was used with 4" Variable Star (page 44), 12" Tall Pines (page 53), and 12" Country Cottage (page 39) blocks.

To add interest, I used a variety of gray fabrics

for the backgrounds around the trees and

houses and two different yellows, so some of

the stars would recede into the lattice strips.

The lattice strips and inner borders were

made using about twenty different fabrics.

QUILT MAP #18

Finished Quilt Size: 80" x 84"
Finished Block Sizes: 4" and 12"
Total Blocks Needed: 33

Yardage Chart (Based on 42" fabric)
Yardage for the actual blocks is not included.

Item	Quantity to Buy
A	2½" SQUARES OF VARIOUS SCRAPS
*Borders & *Binding	2⅜ YARDS
Backing	84" x 88"

*Based on cutting lengthwise grain of the fabric.

Cutting Chart

Item	Cut Size	# To Cut
A	2½" x 2½"	452
Side Borders	6¼" x 74"	2
Top/Bottom Borders	6¼" x 82"	2

tip!

This setting is a scrap lover's dream! It's so simple, yet interesting enough that you will have to take a closer look to see how it was sewn together.

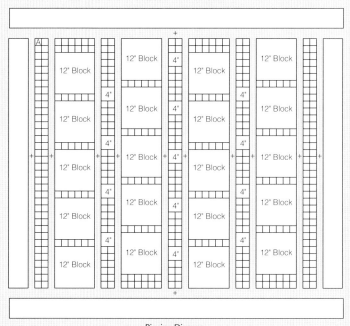

Piecing Diagram

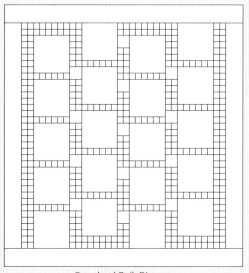

Completed Quilt Diagram

A TABLE RUNNER FOR EVERY OCCASION

17½" x 52½". Made by Nancy Johnson-Srebro.
Quilted by Marcia Stevens.

Quilt Map #19 was used with 12" Pot of Stars (page 62) blocks.

Choose any 12" block and let

the style of the fabric create

the perfect atmosphere for

your dining room or kitchen.

A PLACEMAT FOR EVERY OCCASION

14" x 17½". Made by Nancy Johnson-Srebro.
Quilted by Marcia Stevens.

Quilt Map #20 was used with a 10" Variable Star (page 44) block.

The design of this placemat works

well with the *Table Runner for Every*

Occasion. You could use the same

block in the table runner and place-

mats, or mix and match.

QUILT MAP #19

Finished Quilt Size: 17½" x 52½"
Finished Block Size: 12"
Total Blocks Needed: 2

Yardage Chart (Based on 42" fabric)
Yardage for the actual blocks is not included.

Item	Quantity to Buy
A & B	⅝ YARD
C	¼ YARD
D, *Borders & *Binding	⅞ YARD
Backing	22" x 57"

*Based on cutting crosswise grain of fabric.

Cutting Chart

Item	Cut Size	# To Cut
A	6½" x 21½"	1
B	2" x 2"	56
C	2" x 3½"	28
D	1½" x 12½"	2
**Side Borders	3" x 25"	4
Top/Bottom Borders	3" x 19"	2
Backing	21" x 29"	2

**You will have to piece this border.

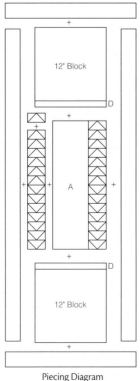

Piecing Diagram

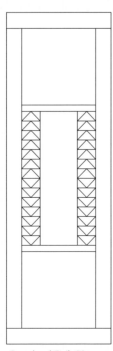

Completed Quilt Diagram

FLYING GEESE SECTION

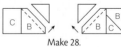

Make 28.

QUILT MAP #20

Finished Quilt Size: 14" x 17½"
Finished Block Size: 10"
Total Blocks Needed: 1

Yardage Chart (Based on 42" fabric)
Yardage for the actual blocks is not included.

Item	Quantity to Buy
A, *Borders & *Binding	⅝ YARD
B	⅛ YARD
C	⅛ YARD
Backing	18" x 22"

*Based on cutting crosswise grain of fabric.

Cutting Chart

Item	Cut Size	# To Cut
A	1½" x 10½"	1
B	1¾" x 1¾"	16
C	1¾" x 3"	8
Side Borders	2¼" x 12"	2
Top/Bottom Borders	2¼" x 19"	2

The flying geese will add a nice touch to any block you use in this placemat.

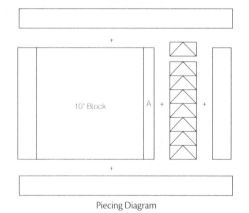

Piecing Diagram

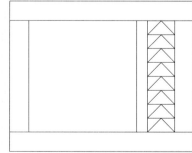

FLYING GEESE SECTION

Make 8.

Completed Quilt Diagram

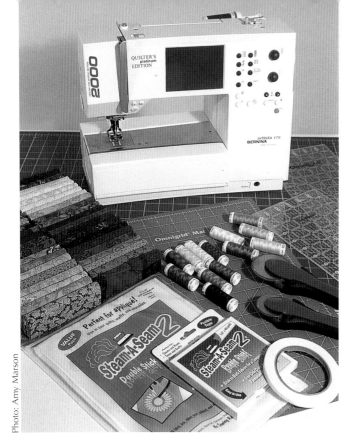

Photo: Amy Marson

RESOURCES

American & Efird, Inc.
Consumer Products Division
400 East Central Avenue
Mt. Holly, NC 28120
www.amefird.com

Benartex, Inc.
1460 Broadway-8th Floor
New York, NY 10036
www.benartex.com

Bernina of America
3500 Thayer Ct.
Aurora, IL 60504
www.berninausa.com

CLOTHWORKS/
Fabric Sales Co., Inc.
6250 Stanley Avenue South
Seattle, WA 98108
www.clothworks-fabric.com

EZ Quilting
85 South Street
West Warren, MA 01092
www.ezquilt.com

Fairfield Processing Corporation
P. O. Box 1130
Danbury, CT 06813
www.poly-fil.com

Mission Valley Fabrics Div. PCCA
980 6th Ave.
New York City, NY 10018
www.missionvalley.com

The Stearns Technical
Textiles Company
100 Williams Street
Cincinnati, OH 45215
www.stearnstextiles.com

P&B Textiles
1580 Gilbreth Road
Burlingame, CA 94010
www.pbtex.com

Prym Dritz/Omnigrid
P. O. Box 5028
Spartanburg, SC 29304
www.dritz.com

Robert Kaufman Co., Inc.
129 W. 132nd Street
Los Angeles, CA 90061
www.robertkaufman.com

RJR Fashion Fabrics
13748 S. Gramercy Place
Gardena, CA 90249
www.rjrfabrics.com

Superior Threads, Inc.
28 East Tabernacle St.
St. George, UT 84770
www.superiorthreads.com

The Warm Company
954 East Union Street
Seattle, WA 98122
www.warmcompany.com

For retail quilting supplies:
Cotton Patch Mail Order
3405 Hall Lane, Dept. CTB
Lafayette, CA 94549
(800) 835-4418
(925) 283-7883
e-mail: quiltusa@yahoo.com
website: www.quiltusa.com

ABOUT THE AUTHOR

Nancy is highly sought after as a quilt-piecing designer, teacher, lecturer and show judge. She has developed No-Fail® methods for accurate rotary cutting and machine piecing.

Nancy has written several books, including: *Miniature To Masterpiece, Featherweight 221—The Perfect Portable®, Measure the Possibilities with Omnigrid, Endless Possibilities,* and *Rotary Magic.* She is also the creator of the "Add On Seam Allowance Chart for Rotary Cutting."

Nancy is president of Silver Star, Inc. and lives in Pennsylvania with her husband, Frank. They have three grown children and one granddaughter, who is already one of her most regular students!

BLOCK MAGIC
CONTEST

CONTEST RULES

Prizes to be Awarded

One **Grand Prize** winner will receive a BERNINA® 150QE sewing machine, valued at $2,299.

One **Second Prize** winner will receive a $500 Shopping Spree at your favorite quilt shop, fabric store, mail-order catalog, or on-line shop. C&T Publishing will present a check for $500 (payable in U.S. dollars) to one retailer of the winner's choice. Winner will be able to purchase any amounts and combinations of products from the chosen retailer up to a total retail value of $500.

One **Third Prize** winner will receive a complete set of Omnigrid® rulers and mats, Dritz cutters, and Omnigrid bag, valued at $300.

Five **Honorable Mention** winners will receive a Nancy Johnson-Srebro Goodie Bag, valued at $200 each, containing fabric, threads, stencils, batting, and quilting notions from Benartex Inc., Mettler and Signature by American & Efird, Inc., The Stencil Company, The Warm™ Company, and Collins.

Special Category for Shop Owners: One winning shop owner will receive a $300 merchandise credit from C&T Publishing.

Special Category for Shop Owners

• Create a Block of the Month plan for your customers from *Block Magic* and enter a photo of the finished shop quilt. Please follow "How to Enter" instructions above. (The same rules for "Eligibility" and "Awarding of Prizes" also apply to this category.)

• One winning shop owner will receive a $300 merchandise credit from C&T Publishing.

• Winner in the Shop Owners Category will be chosen by C&T Publishing and Nancy Johnson-Srebro.

How to Enter

Please do not send in your quilt; photos only.

All entries must include:

a) A photo of the finished quilt you have created based on a pattern or patterns from *Block Magic* by Nancy Johnson-Srebro. Please clearly label your photo with your name, address, and telephone number. The submission can be a photo or slide (see tips at www.ctpub.com on "How to Take Good Photos"), or it can be sent as an e-mail attachment (see "Attachment Tips" at www.ctpub.com).

b) The following additional information: which pattern or patterns you used from *Block Magic*; the size of your quilt; your name and the names of everyone who worked on the quilt; your complete mailing address; your telephone number; the name and address of your favorite quilt shop, fabric store, mail-order catalog, or on-line shop; your fax number and e-mail address (if available).

E-Mail Entries: E-mail your entry to ctinfo@ctpub.com, and include the words "Block Magic Contest Entry" in the subject box. Entry information should be entered in the body of the e-mail, and photos should be included as an attachment (see "Attachment Tips" at www.ctpub.com). E-mail entries must be received no later than 5:00 p.m. (Pacific Time), January 15, 2002.

Mail-In Entries: Send entries to "Block Magic Contest," c/o C&T Publishing, Inc., 1651 Challenge Drive, Concord, CA 94520. Mail-in entries must be postmarked by January 15, 2002 and received no later than 5:00 p.m. (Pacific Time), January 24, 2002.

Awarding of Prizes

• Eight semi-finalist quilts will be selected by a jury from all entries received by the deadline date as described above. Semi-finalist quilts will be selected based on the creative use of block(s) from *Block Magic* and the overall effect of the quilt.

• Starting February 1, 2002, semi-finalist quilts will be posted on the C&T Publishing website (www.ctpub.com). From February 1, 2002 through April 1, 2002, website visitors can vote for their favorite semi-finalist (one vote per visitor allowed—multiple entries will be eliminated).

• The semi-finalist quilt with the most votes will be the Grand Prize winner; the semi-finalist quilt with the second highest number of votes will be the Second Prize winner; and the semi-finalist quilt with the third highest number of votes will be the Third Prize winner. The remaining five semi-finalists will receive the Honorable Mention prizes.

• Special Category for Shop Owners winner will be selected by C&T Publishing and Nancy Johnson-Srebro.

• Winners will be announced by April 15, 2002.

• The decisions of the contest jury in choosing the semi-finalists and the tally of the on-line votes are final.

• No substitution in prizes will be allowed, and the prizes may not be redeemed for cash or other consideration.

• Winners will be notified by telephone or mail by April 30, 2002.

• All prizes will be awarded and distributed on or before May 31, 2002.

• Odds of winning are incalculable and depend on the number of eligible entries received by the deadline date.

• Winners are solely responsible for all taxes where applicable. The Second Prize winner is solely responsible for any costs related to visiting or ordering from the chosen retailer.

• For a notice of contest winners, send a self-addressed stamped envelope to the contest sponsor: "Block Magic Contest Winner," C&T Publishing, Inc., 1651 Challenge Drive, Concord, CA 94520, or visit our website at www.ctpub.com.

Eligibility

No purchase is required to enter.

• One entry per person. (See "How to Enter" section for instructions. Please do not send in your quilt; photos only.)

• Contest is open to anyone in the United States except employees of the contest sponsors, their family members, and those excluded as stated within the eligibility requirements listed below.

• By submitting an entry, participant agrees to the use of his or her name, city and state, quilt, and photograph for advertising/publicity purposes without compensation and allow sponsors to send promotional information. Furthermore, participation gives sponsors the non-exclusive right to reproduce the quilt in any and all future publications and for promotional purposes.

• Winners must agree to promptly sign an Affidavit of Eligibility. The Second Prize winner's chosen retailer must promptly sign a receipt for the $500 check.

• All entries become the property of C&T Publishing, Inc. and the contest jury. Photographs submitted will not be returned.

• Each quilt entered must be constructed and quilted by the person or persons named in the submitted entry.

• This contest is void where prohibited by law.

• Contest begins at 12:01 a.m. (Pacific Time), May 1, 2001, and entries must be postmarked or e-mailed by January 15, 2002, 5:00 p.m. (Pacific Time).

• Contest sponsors are not responsible for late, lost, incomplete, or illegible entries.

• Entries must be complete for consideration.